THE ESSENTIAL
RICE COOKER
COOKBOOK

Take Your Appliance Beyond the Rice

with 60 Complete Meals Made Perfect Every Time

SHREE MITRA

creator of TruffleandToast

PAGE STREET
PUBLISHING CO.

First published in 2022 by
Page Street Publishing Co.
27 Congress Street, Suite 1511
Salem, MA 01970
www.pagestreetpublishing.com

Distributed by Macmillan, sales in Canada by The Canadian Manda Group.

26 25 24 23 22   1 2 3 4 5

ISBN-13: 978-1-64567-588-4
ISBN-10: 1-64567-588-2

Library of Congress Control Number: 2021952288

Cover and book design by Molly Kate Young for Page Street Publishing Co.
Photography by Ha Le and Shree Mitra

Printed and bound in The United States of America

DEDICATION

This book is dedicated to my parents,
who have loved me unconditionally, been my
constant source of support and sacrificed so much
for my happiness. Everything I am today
and may become tomorrow, I owe to you.

CONTENTS

INTRODUCTION

Do you own a rice cooker and haven't used it for anything beyond cooking rice? Or worse, were you gifted one that is sitting on your shelf gathering dust because you don't know what to do with it? Or, maybe you are planning to invest in a rice cooker but aren't able to decide if it's worth it?

Then you'll be glad to know that the rice cooker isn't just a one-hit wonder. While it makes perfectly fluffy rice each time, you can also use it to cook a variety of soups, entrées, curries, noodles and even desserts! For breakfast, you can indulge in a plate of Fluffy Pancakes with Berries and Cream (page 138) or a sweet bowl of Autumnal Apple Pie Oatmeal (page 142). Whip up some Milk-Poached Cod with Leeks (page 112) or a Tasty Sri Lankan Dal Parippu (Coconut Lentil Curry; page 92) for a light lunch. Go all out with Fall Pumpkin Risotto (page 17) or a Moroccan Chicken Tagine (page 78) for dinner. There are so many delicious and exciting meals that can be made in the rice cooker, and with this book I'll show you how!

I was really excited when my publishers got in touch with me to work on a cookbook. I have been food blogging for over 7 years now. When I first started my page, I was mainly using it as a platform to share my recommendations for London's best restaurants and street food spots with my audience. But as time went on, I started to get invited by restaurants to review their food and before I realized it, I was eating out every single day and reviewing eight to ten restaurants a week. This was definitely a fantastic and exhilarating experience, but not very sustainable, as you might imagine. Therefore, I decided to have home-cooked meals at least a few days every week to give my body a bit of a detox.

When it comes to cooking, I want to eat varied, flavor-packed dishes, but I don't usually have hours to slog away in the kitchen. So, most of my recipes tend to be tasty, quick and put together in less than 30 minutes. I enjoy making comforting bowls of pasta just as much as recreating more elaborate dishes from some of my favorite London restaurants. My cooking is also influenced by my Indian heritage. Many of the dishes I make are inspired by my mum's recipes. I have included a range of these recipes in the book, such as the Steamed Cod in Mustard Sauce (page 115), Ma's Moong Dal Khichdi (page 24) and the Mughlai Keema Matar (page 75).

My publishers and I went back and forth on the concept for my book, and I am so thrilled that in the end we went ahead with rice cooker recipes. I'm all about low-effort, nourishing recipes, and the rice cooker is perfect for that, as you'll see throughout this book.

I first bought a rice cooker when I was in university, and it was a real savior. Making rice is actually pretty difficult. You need to get the right water-to-rice ratio, cook it at the correct temperature and know when to turn off the stove. So, unsurprisingly, I've had mushy rice, scorched rice and crunchy rice, but thankfully, the rice cooker came to the rescue, and I haven't stopped using it since! No more waiting by the stove. No more juggling grain or protein timings. Just easy, expertly cooked rice every time.

The way a rice cooker works is by gradually heating the grains and then switching off the heat when the liquid is fully absorbed. For most rice cookers, this happens at 212°F (100°C), which is the boiling point of water, and the process typically takes between 20 and 30 minutes.

While the recipes in this book have been developed to work in a variety of rice cookers, it is common for different brands of rice cookers to vary slightly in cooking times, rice-to-water ratio and functionality, so it's very important to read the instructions that come with your rice cooker. You might also need to slightly tailor the timings or the amount of liquid being added to the recipes provided in this book to your specific rice cooker. I personally use a Russell Hobbs Rice Cooker and Steamer 1.8L, which is a no-frills cooker with just one button—but it does the job just fine!

Not only is the rice cooker versatile in the range of dishes you can make using it, but also most of the dishes are one-pot, fuss-free recipes. So, you need to spend a lot less time manning your dish when cooking with the rice cooker—just pick the recipe, throw in the ingredients, set the cooker to Cook and let the magic happen while you do the laundry or catch up on your favorite show!

Any slow-cooked dishes that require being simmered over a long time can be made in a rice cooker with delicious results, like stews and casseroles. The rice cooker works equally well as a steamer or poacher, making it an ideal way of cooking fish, steaming tofu or making dumplings. But perhaps the most interesting discovery for me was realizing that the rice cooker pot can also act as a fairly functional fry pan. Now it isn't really suited to dishes that require very high temperatures like deep frying or caramelizing, but you can easily sauté onions, panfry chicken and cook ground meat in the rice cooker pot.

Technically you can also bake cakes in the rice cooker pot, but I did find that it required several cooking cycles, which makes the experience less enjoyable. I decided to only feature recipes in this book that are genuinely worth preparing in the rice cooker without too many additional steps, like portions being prepared on the stove, in a slow cooker or in an oven.

It's been so much fun working on this book, and it's honestly such a privilege for me to be able to share dishes from my childhood and those inspired by my restaurant escapades in London. Whether you've already got a rice cooker or are planning to get one, I hope the recipes in this book will inspire you and encourage you to experiment. I'll be doing a happy dance for every person that walks away seeing the rice cooker as more than something to just cook rice in!

Shreedipta Mitra

RICE COOKER TIPS AND TRICKS

Here are a few of my general tips and tricks for using a rice cooker that I think you'll find helpful as you navigate this cookbook:

- All rice cookers have at least two basic modes: Cook and Warm. The Cook mode is when the rice cooker is operating at a higher temperature—this is the mode you will use to do most of your cooking, steaming and frying. The Warm mode is useful when your dish is mostly done but you want to slow cook to get your meat tender or to round off the flavors.

- Many of my recipes require you to preheat the rice cooker before you begin cooking or to heat oil in the rice cooker to sauté spices. Usually, you will find that the rice cooker doesn't stay in the Cook mode when the weight of the ingredients is too low or if the pot is empty. What you need to do in these cases is to simply put on the lid! Adding the lid presses the pot down on the thermal sensing element, so you will then be able to switch to the Cook mode easily.

- The rice cooker can sometimes switch to the Warm mode if it gets too hot or if most of the liquid inside has evaporated. In these scenarios, simply wait for a few minutes before switching it back to Cook if the recipe needs any more cooking time.

- If you wash out the rice cooker pot between the recipe steps, make sure to dry it fully before placing it back on the heating plate. This is essential to prevent the device from malfunctioning and to avoid any risk of electric shock.

- If your rice cooker doesn't come with a steamer basket or tray (though most models do), you can use a cooling rack, a colander or even a heat-proof plate placed on some aluminum foil balls. If you're going ahead with the foil and plate method, just make sure that the plate is smaller in diameter than the pot, so you can easily place it inside and lift it out once the steaming is done.

- Wherever I use the term "simmer", I am referring to the rice cooker being set to Warm mode.

RICE-BASED ENTRÉES

How could one possibly have a rice cooker cookbook without an assortment of rice dishes? If you own a rice cooker, you are probably already using it to make some good old-fashioned steamed rice to go with your meals, but I wanted to share some more exciting rice-based recipes from around the world, which I have loved eating and making over the years.

Rice is a fantastic blank canvas for flavors. It may not be as trendy as quinoa or barley but I've always loved rice-based recipes. Soft, hot-off-the-stove and fluffy, this humble pantry item is just so versatile. You can have it stuffed in a burrito, layered into sushi rolls or added to a comforting casserole.

I hope that the recipes in this chapter will show you that rice doesn't have to be a side dish—it can very much be the headline act. Many of these dishes can also be wonderful for meal prep. Just throw the spices and vegetables into the rice cooker pot with the rice and let the magic happen—lunch is sorted for the next few days with minimal cleaning and effort! In this chapter, we've got everything from Fiery Jollof Rice (page 21) to Decadent Chicken Biryani (page 31) and cozy Fall Pumpkin Risotto (page 17) covered. So, you've just got to choose your first recipe and get cooking!

CREOLE CHORIZO AND PRAWN JAMBALAYA

Jambalaya is a wonderfully comforting and flavorful rice dish with varying stories of origin. The dish has some similarity to the Spanish paella but also includes French and African influences. While differing from one household to another, there are two main recipes we know of: Creole and Cajun. The Creole version of the dish tends to include tomatoes, which give it a reddish hue, while the Cajun version involves caramelizing the meat, giving it a smokier flavor and a browner color. The recipe below is an easy spin on the Creole jambalaya. Making it in the rice cooker will ensure that it is moist and flavorsome without being soupy, because even if you put in a bit too much or too little of the broth, the cooker will adjust to give you perfectly fluffy rice.

Yield: 2–3 servings

1½ tbsp (21 g) unsalted butter

1 cup (160 g) diced white onions

5 oz (140 g) red bell pepper, diced

2 tbsp (17 g) minced garlic

7 oz (200 g) chorizo, sliced

¾ cup (150 g) white rice

2 cups (480 ml) chicken broth

7 oz (200 g) chopped plum tomatoes

1 tsp paprika

¼ tsp freshly ground black pepper

2 tsp (2 g) Cajun seasoning

7 oz (200 g) frozen prawns, tails on

¼ cup (30 g) chopped fresh parsley

Salt, to taste

2 tbsp (6 g) finely sliced scallions, to serve

Turn on the rice cooker, set the mode to Cook and add the lid to let the rice cooker preheat for about 1 minute. Once it has heated up, remove the lid. Then add the butter and spread it evenly over the base of the cooker.

Once the butter melts, which will take 30 seconds to a minute, add the onions and bell pepper and sauté them until they're tender. This should take 4 to 5 minutes. You can do this step with the lid off, but if you find that the cooker auto-switches to the Warm mode, just put the lid on and turn it back to the Cook mode. You can then remove the lid after 2 to 3 minutes, give it all a good stir and then put the lid back on.

Once the vegetables are tender, remove the lid and add the garlic and chorizo. Sauté them until everything is well-browned, which should take another 5 to 6 minutes.

When the garlic and chorizo are browned, add the rice to the rice cooker and stir. Then pour in the broth and tomatoes, and stir in the paprika, ground pepper and Cajun seasoning. Mix everything together well and put on the lid.

Cook the meal for 15 to 20 minutes, or until the rice is nearly done. Then remove the lid and add the prawns. Put the lid back on and cook for another 4 to 5 minutes, or until the prawns are pink and fully cooked through.

Remove the lid to stir in the parsley and salt, if desired. Put the lid back on and set the rice cooker to the Warm mode for another 5 minutes or until you are ready to serve.

Serve the jambalaya topped with chopped scallions.

FALL PUMPKIN RISOTTO

Creamy risottos are an embodiment of Italian home cooking: elegant, yet comforting. One of its most celebrated forms is Risotto Alla Zucca, or pumpkin risotto, which is particularly popular in Lombardy in northern Italy due to the huge quantities of gorgeous pumpkins grown in the area.

Typically, pumpkin risotto is garnished with sage, but I remember trying this incredible version in Tuscany with just a few drops of thick balsamic vinegar, aged for 20 years. The sweetness of the balsamic enhances the pumpkin while the slight tartness cuts through the richness of the cheese. Even if you can't get something that aged, balsamic that's even 10 to 12 years old will work beautifully.

Also, there'll be no need to constantly stir your risotto in a rice cooker, unlike on the stove, saving you a lot of time and hassle.

Yield: 4 servings

1 tbsp (15 ml) olive oil

1 tbsp (14 g) unsalted butter

½ cup (80 g) chopped white onions

1½ cups (300 g) Arborio rice

3 cups (720 ml) chicken stock, plus more if needed

12 oz (340 g) pumpkin, peeled, de-seeded and diced

½ tsp nutmeg

½ tsp freshly ground black pepper

¾ cup (25 g) grated Parmesan

Salt, to taste

1 tsp aged balsamic vinegar, to serve

Shaved Parmesan, to serve

Turn on the rice cooker, set the mode to Cook and put on the lid to let the rice cooker preheat for about 1 minute. Once it has heated up, remove the lid. Then add the olive oil and butter and spread them evenly over the base of the cooker. Put the lid back on and cook for 30 seconds to a minute, or until the butter melts. Then remove the lid, toss in the onions and sauté them for 3 to 4 minutes, or until they're soft and just starting to turn golden brown. If the rice cooker auto-switches to Warm while frying the onions, just put the lid on and set it back to Cook, giving them a stir midway through cooking.

Now add the rice and stir to ensure all the grains are coated in the butter and onions. Stir everything together for 2 to 3 minutes.

Once the onions are softened and starting to turn golden, pour in the stock, add the pumpkin and stir them to combine. Put the lid on and cook for 25 to 30 minutes, stirring midway through.

Remove the lid and stir in the nutmeg, pepper and Parmesan and cook for 1 to 2 minutes. Add some more stock if needed, aiming for a creamy consistency. Add some salt, if desired. Put the lid back on. Turn the rice cooker mode to Warm and keep it on this setting until you're ready to serve.

Serve the meal with a drizzle of balsamic vinegar and some shaved Parmesan.

EASY SMOKED HADDOCK KEDGEREE

Kedgeree is a wholesome, buttery dish combining curried rice, flaky smoked fish and gooey eggs, which can be eaten hot or cold. If you think these flavors sound like a bit of fusion, you'd be right! Kedgeree originated in India, and a simplified version was introduced to the United Kingdom by the returning British colonials as a breakfast dish. According to the former royal family chef, Darren McGrady, the dish was a firm favorite for Prince Philip and Queen Elizabeth. I don't know about you, but I feel that if it's good enough for the Queen, it's good enough for me!

 Yield: 2 servings

2–3 medium eggs

9 oz (255 g) smoked haddock fillet

2 bay leaves

¾ cup (180 ml) whole milk

2 tbsp (28 g) unsalted butter

1 tbsp (15 ml) olive oil

¼ cup (40 g) finely sliced white onions

2 tsp (6 g) minced garlic

2 tsp (4 g) curry powder

1½ cups (150 g) basmati rice

2 cups (480 ml) fish stock or water

To boil the eggs, add 3 cups (720 ml) of water to the rice cooker. Add the lid and set the rice cooker to Cook. Give it 8 to 10 minutes, or until the water comes to a rolling boil. Remove the lid and place the eggs in the steamer basket. Add the lid and steam the eggs for 6½ minutes (we want them to be soft and jammy). While your eggs are steaming, add ice and water to a small mixing bowl. When your 6½ minutes are up, move the eggs to the bowl of ice water to stop them from cooking any further. Set them aside. Turn the rice cooker off and discard the remaining water from the rice cooker pot.

Turn the rice cooker back on. Place the smoked haddock fillet and bay leaves in the rice cooker pot. Cover them with the milk. Add the rice cooker lid and set it to the Cook setting for 10 to 12 minutes, or until the fish flakes easily. Turn the cooker off. Strain the liquid and reserve it; we will use this to cook the rice later on. Flake the fish, then set it aside and keep it warm. Remove and discard the bay leaves.

Wash out and dry the pan completely. Turn on the rice cooker, set the mode to Cook and add the lid to let the rice cooker preheat for about 1 minute. Next, add the butter and olive oil. Once the butter has melted, which will take about 30 seconds to 1 minute, remove the lid and add in the onions. Add the lid back on and cook for 6 to 8 minutes, or until they're softened. Now add in the garlic and fry it for 1 minute more, or until golden. Stir in the curry powder and rice and toss well. Fry everything for 3 to 4 minutes, or until it's aromatic, and then pour in the poaching liquid and the stock. With the lid on, cook the mixture for 20 to 25 minutes, or until the rice is almost tender.

(continued)

4 oz (115 g) frozen peas

3 tbsp (10 g) finely chopped flat-leaf parsley, plus more to serve

4 tbsp (60 ml) heavy cream

Salt, to taste

1 lemon, cut into wedges, to serve

At this stage, remove the lid, add the peas to the rice and cook for another 5 to 6 minutes with the lid on. Meanwhile, peel the eggs, quarter them and set them aside.

Remove the lid and gently stir in the flaked haddock, parsley and heavy cream until they're combined.

Add some salt and change the rice cooker mode to Warm. Keep the lid on and keep the dish in the rice cooker until you're ready to serve the meal.

When serving, top the dish with the eggs, additional parsley and lemon wedges.

FIERY JOLLOF RICE

No party in Africa is complete without this spicy rice dish, simmered in an aromatic blend of onions, tomatoes and peppers. Ghana and Nigeria make the two most popular varieties of jollof rice. Ghanaians use fragrant basmati rice while Nigerians use sturdier long-grain rice, which is better at absorbing flavors from the tomato stew base. The recipe below is inspired by the Ghanaian jollof.

Traditionally, the recipe features a ton of scotch bonnet peppers, giving you a fantastically flavorsome yet extremely hot dish. Thankfully, the dish also works with fewer scotch bonnets or even milder red chilies to taste.

Jollof rice definitely takes a bit of love and care, but using the rice cooker means that you don't have to worry about it burning, and washing up after cooking will be easy.

 Yield: 4 servings

For the Tomato Puree

1 tbsp (15 ml) palm oil

1 cup (160 g) chopped yellow onions

1 tsp salt

1 tsp curry powder

1 tsp smoked paprika

2 tbsp (17 g) chopped garlic

2 tsp (5 g) chopped fresh ginger

1–2 scotch bonnet chilies, seeded and chopped (add more/less to your taste)

1 (6-oz [170-g]) can tomato paste

12 oz (340 g) canned diced tomatoes

To make the tomato puree, turn on the rice cooker and allow it to preheat by setting it to Cook and covering it with the lid. Once it has heated up, which should take 1 to 2 minutes, remove the lid, add the palm oil and put the lid back on. Let the oil heat up for a minute.

Add in the onions and season them with salt, curry powder and smoked paprika. Sauté them for a minute and then add the lid. Fry for 4 to 5 minutes, or until the onions become translucent. Next, add the garlic, ginger and chilies and cook for another 2 to 3 minutes, or until they are fragrant.

Now add the tomato paste and mix it in well. Cover and cook for another 4 to 5 minutes. Then turn the rice cooker off. Let the mixture cool slightly, and then transfer all the ingredients to a blender along with the diced tomatoes. Blend until the mixture is smooth then set it aside.

(continued)

For the Rice

¼ cup (60 ml) olive oil

¼ cup (40 g) chopped red onions

2 tsp (5 g) minced garlic

1 tsp grated fresh ginger

3 oz (85 g) red bell pepper, diced

2 cups (400 g) jasmine rice, rinsed and drained

½ cup (70 g) frozen peas

⅓ cup (55 g) canned sweet corn, drained

½ cup (65 g) finely diced carrots

1 tbsp (6 g) curry powder

½ tbsp (4 g) smoked sweet paprika

1 tsp dried thyme

1 tsp kosher salt

1 tsp freshly ground black pepper

1 bay leaf

1½ cups (360 ml) water, plus more if needed

Fresh coriander and sliced red onions, to serve

To make the jollof rice, turn the rice cooker back on. In the rice cooker pot, heat the olive oil with the lid on and with the device set to Cook. The oil should take a minute to heat up. Once it's shimmering, add in the onions, garlic and ginger. Cover and cook for 5 to 6 minutes, or until they're slightly browned. Stir midway through. Now add the bell pepper and cook for another 3 to 4 minutes with the lid on.

Remove the lid. Then toss in the rice, peas, sweet corn, carrots, curry powder, paprika, thyme, salt and pepper. Stir for 3 to 4 minutes until the rice is fragrant. Add in the bay leaf and water. Cover and cook for 15 to 20 minutes, stirring midway through. Once most of the liquid has been absorbed, pour in the prepared tomato puree and cook, with the lid back on, until the rice is tender, which should take 10 to 12 minutes.

If the rice looks too dry, feel free to add an additional ½ cup (120 ml) of water and stir it in. Change the rice cooker mode to Warm and let the rice sit for at least 5 minutes, or until you're ready to serve it. Remove the bay leaf and fluff the rice before serving it garnished with fresh coriander and sliced onions.

MA'S MOONG DAL KHICHDI (INDIAN LENTIL AND RICE STEW)

Khichdi is synonymous with comfort food in India. This staple Indian dish uses only pantry items, is super easy to prepare and is so nourishing. In its most basic form, khichdi is simply lentils and rice cooked to a porridge-like texture. However, the recipe below is far more complex and flavorsome and it is how my mum makes it. I sauté the lentils before cooking them for a slightly nutty taste. The carrots, peas and beans make the khichdi colorful and nutritious, while ginger and cumin add aroma. The ghee makes it a lot more indulgent. I might be biased, but I do think this really is the tastiest way to eat khichdi, and I am confident that after you've tried it, you'll be a fan too!

◆—— Yield: 2 servings ——◆

½ cup (100 g) moong dal (split and husked mung beans)

½ cup (100 g) basmati rice

3 tbsp (45 g) ghee, divided

1 tsp cumin seeds

1 bay leaf

⅓ cup (55 g) finely chopped red onions

1 tsp grated fresh ginger

½ cup (90 g) chopped plum tomatoes

½ tsp chopped green chilies

½ cup (65 g) diced carrots

¼ cup (35 g) frozen peas

¼ tsp turmeric powder

½ tsp red chili powder

3 cups (720 ml) water

Salt, to taste

¼ tsp asafoetida (hing) (optional; see Note)

Rinse and wash the moong dal and rice in separate bowls. Soak the dal and rice for 30 minutes in water in their own bowls. After 30 minutes, drain all the water and set the dal and rice aside.

Turn the rice cooker on, set it to Cook and add the lid. Let the rice cooker preheat for 1 to 2 minutes and then add in 2 tablespoons (30 ml) of ghee. Place the lid back on and cook for another minute, or until the ghee melts. Once the ghee has melted, remove the lid and add in the cumin seeds, bay leaf, onions and ginger. Sauté them for a minute and then put the lid back on.

Fry for 2 to 3 minutes, or until the onions are translucent. Then remove the lid and add the dal. Fry for 2 more minutes, or until the ingredients are lightly fragrant. Next, throw in the tomatoes and chilies. Sauté them for 2 to 3 minutes, or until the tomatoes soften.

Next, add the carrots, peas, turmeric, chili powder and rice. Pour in 3 cups (720 ml) of water, mix well and then add salt. Also add in the asafoetida at this stage if you are planning to use it.

Cover and cook for 25 to 30 minutes, or until the rice and dal are fully cooked. Remove the bay leaf before serving the khichdi with 1 tablespoon (15 g) of ghee.

NOTE: *I have kept the asafoetida optional as it does have an intense aroma, but a pinch of it can help balance out the flavors in a dish. Asafoetida, or hing, comes from the resin of giant fennel plants and adds a hint of umami to the dish. You can find this spice in Indian supermarkets or online.*

AUTHENTIC CHINESE STICKY RICE

There is something so incredibly satisfying about deeply flavorful and sticky, chewy grains of rice. I love having it at dim sum spreads, as well as for a comforting lunch at home. In this dish, I really love the spectacular flavors you get from the shiitake mushrooms, Chinese sausage, oyster sauce and soy sauce with the tender and soft, sticky rice.

The most essential step to getting this dish right is buying the right kind of rice. You want to use short-grain glutinous or sweet rice, which is a lot stickier than regular rice. Typically, you'd need to soak the glutinous rice for 2 to 3 hours or ideally overnight to soften the grains and reduce cooking time but with rice cookers, that much soaking time isn't required, meaning much less prep time!

 Yield: 4 servings

For the Sauce

3 tbsp (45 ml) oyster sauce

1 tbsp (15 ml) soy sauce

1 tsp grated fresh ginger

1 tsp minced garlic

½ tsp cornstarch

½ tsp sesame oil

¼ tsp ground white pepper

For the Rice

2–3 medium-sized dried shiitake mushrooms, soaked in hot water for at least 20 minutes

1 tbsp (15 ml) peanut or vegetable oil

½ lb (225 g) ground pork

4 oz (115 g) Lap Cheong Chinese sausages, sliced (see Note)

2 cups (400 g) glutinous rice, soaked in water for 30 minutes

1¼ cups (300 ml) water

2 tsp (2 g) chopped scallions, to serve

To make the sauce, in a small bowl, mix the oyster sauce, soy sauce, ginger, garlic, cornstarch, sesame oil and white pepper and set it aside.

To begin the rice dish, remove the mushrooms from the water they have been soaking in and squeeze out some of the liquid. Cut off the stems of the mushrooms. Dice the rest and set them aside.

Turn the rice cooker on and set it to Cook. Put the lid on and let the rice cooker preheat for a minute. Then add in the peanut oil and heat it, covered, for 1 to 2 minutes. Once it heats up, add the ground pork and the Chinese sausages. Cook them for 5 to 6 minutes, or until the pork is mostly cooked through. Then add the shiitake mushrooms. Fry them for a minute.

Drain the glutinous rice and add it to the pot as a layer above the pork. Don't mix it in. Pour in the water. Close the lid and cook for 25 to 30 minutes, until the rice is completely cooked. Mix well before serving. Portion the meal out into bowls and top with chopped scallions.

NOTE: *Chinese sausage is an umbrella term for a range of different smoked and air-cured meats from different parts of China which are usually made with pork, liver, pork fat and chicken. This recipe calls for Lap Cheong which is a bit sweeter than the Sichuan and Hunan ones. You can find it in most local Chinese supermarkets but other types of Chinese sausage will also work if you can't find Lap Cheong.*

PRETTY PINEAPPLE FRIED RICE

If there is one dish that transports me to a sunny Thai beach, it would have to be this one. I love how well the sweet, juicy pineapple pieces go with the savory curry powder and garlicky Jasmine rice. The dish bursts with all the fantastic flavors of aromatic onions, buttery cashews and fragrant scallions. I use a fresh, whole pineapple so I can use the flesh and also use it for serving the fried rice but if you're in a rush, you can also use canned pineapple chunks. I know that you might have reservations about fruit in fried rice, but once you try this dish, I guarantee all your apprehension will be well and truly dispelled!

⤙ Yield: 2 servings (see Note) ⤚

1 whole pineapple

2 tbsp (28 g) unsalted butter

¼ cup (35 g) roasted and unsalted cashews, plus a few to serve

½ cup (120 ml) vegetable oil, divided

2 medium eggs, beaten with a dash of salt

½ lb (225 g) prawns, shelled, deveined and with the tails removed

First prep the pineapple—this is perhaps the only slightly tricky part of the recipe. Slice the pineapple in half (lengthwise). Use a sharp knife to cut around the edge of the pineapple, being careful not to cut through its skin. Cut the pineapple flesh in the middle into small cubes and then scoop them out using a spoon. Remove the core pieces and set the rest aside for later.

Turn on the rice cooker, set the mode to Cook and add the lid to let it preheat for about 1 minute. Add the butter to the rice cooker pot, put the lid on and set it to Cook. The butter will take 1 to 2 minutes to heat up. As the butter melts, toss in the cashews and fry them for 1 to 2 minutes, or until they're golden on each side. Remove them from the pot and set them aside.

Next, add 1 tablespoon (15 ml) of the vegetable oil, cover and set to Cook for a minute. Once the oil heats up, add in the beaten eggs and stir-fry for 1 to 2 minutes, or until they are scrambled. Set them aside.

Add in another tablespoon (15 ml) of the oil to the rice cooker and heat it for 1 to 2 minutes with the lid closed. Once it's hot, add in the prawns. Fry the prawns, covered, for 4 to 5 minutes, or until they are cooked through and opaque.

(continued)

¼ cup (40 g) finely chopped red onions

5 tsp (15 g) minced garlic

1 tsp finely diced fresh red chili

¼ cup (40 g) canned sweet corn, drained

¼ cup (35 g) canned peas, drained

¼ cup (32 g) diced carrots

¼ cup (12 g) sliced scallions, plus 1 tbsp (3 g) to serve

2 cups (200 g) jasmine or any long-grain rice, cooked

1 tbsp (15 ml) soy sauce, or to taste

1 tbsp (6 g) curry powder

1 tsp fish sauce, or to taste

2 tbsp (30 ml) lime juice

Once the prawns are cooked, set them aside and add the remaining 6 tablespoons (90 ml) of oil to the pot. Let it heat up in the cooker with the lid on for a minute. Throw in the onions, sauté them for 1 to 2 minutes and then put the lid on. Fry the onions for 3 to 4 minutes more, or until they are softened. Now add in the garlic and red chilies and sauté them for 1 to 2 minutes, or until the garlic is fragrant.

Toss in the sweet corn, peas, carrots and scallions. Fry them for 30 seconds and then add in the cooked rice. Season the dish with the soy sauce and curry powder and give it all a good mix. Fry for 5 to 6 minutes more, until the vegetables are cooked.

Throw the scrambled eggs and fried prawns into the rice. Drizzle the fish sauce and lime juice over everything. Toss well and put the fried rice into the pineapple halves. Serve it with some more scallions and fried cashews.

NOTE: This recipe can serve up to 4, if you would prefer to serve it in regular bowls instead of in the two pineapple halves.

DECADENT CHICKEN BIRYANI

This is a dish you'll find at every Indian wedding. A biryani is a wonderfully aromatic, intricate dish, involving layers of braised meat, parboiled rice, warming spices and caramelized onions that traditionally takes around 6 to 12 hours to make. But here's a cheat version that you can whip up in one pot with much less prep while not compromising on taste.

The distinct flavor of biryani is predominantly due to the generous amount of whole spices that go in. Traditionally, we discard the spices while eating, but you can pop them all in a muslin bag before frying to avoid biting into them. Though sides are optional, I'm serving mine with some raita made by mixing Greek yogurt with grated cucumber, lime juice and garam masala.

⟵ Yield: 2–3 servings ⟶

For the Chicken Marinade

⅔ cup (200 g) plain Greek yogurt

1 tsp minced garlic

1 tsp grated fresh ginger

1 tsp Kashmiri chili powder

1 tsp garam masala

1 tsp whole cumin seeds, crushed

1 tsp turmeric

½ tsp salt

1 tsp lemon juice

2 tbsp (30 ml) vegetable oil

1 tbsp (1 g) fresh coriander

1 tsp sliced green chilies

1 lb (450 g) bone-in chicken thighs and drumsticks

For the Saffron Milk

¼ tsp saffron

1 tbsp (15 ml) whole milk

1 tbsp (15 ml) hot water

To make the marinade, place all of the ingredients for the marinade in a big bowl: yogurt, garlic, ginger, Kashmiri chili powder, garam masala, crushed cumin, turmeric, salt, lemon juice, vegetable oil, coriander and chilies. Mix the ingredients well, then add the chicken. Refrigerate the mixture for 2 to 3 hours to let the chicken marinate. You could also do this step the night before you plan to make the biryani. The longer the chicken is marinated, the more tender and flavorsome it will be.

For the saffron milk, in a small bowl, grind the saffron threads and then add the milk and 1 tablespoon (15 ml) of hot water. Set it aside to infuse while you do the rest of the prep.

(continued)

For the Biryani

1½ cups (300 g) basmati rice

5 tbsp (75 g) ghee, divided

2 cups (320 g) thinly sliced red onions

2 bay leaves

6 green cardamom pods

2 black cardamom pods

1 tsp black peppercorn

1 star anise

1 cinnamon stick

1 tsp cumin seeds

2½ cups (600 ml) water

2 tbsp (30 ml) rose water

½ tsp kewra water (see Note)

2 tbsp (2 g) fresh coriander, to serve

Lemon slices, to serve

To begin the biryani, wash the rice three to four times and then leave it to soak for at least 30 minutes. Turn on the rice cooker, set the mode to Cook and add the lid to let the rice cooker preheat for about 1 minute. Add 3 tablespoons (45 g) of ghee to the rice cooker pot. Put the lid on and let the ghee heat up, which will take 1 to 2 minutes. Once the ghee melts, add the onions. Sauté them for 1 to 2 minutes and then add the lid again. Fry for 12 to 15 minutes, or until the onions begin to brown. Remove the lid. Take the onions out and set them aside.

Add 1 tablespoon (15 g) of ghee to the pot along with the whole spices: bay leaves, green cardamom pods, black cardamom pods, black peppercorns, star anise, cinnamon stick and cumin seeds. Fry them for 1 to 2 minutes, or until they're fragrant. Then add the marinated chicken and place the lid on. Fry the chicken for 3 to 4 minutes, or until it is lightly browned. Lift the lid, turn the chicken pieces over and fry them for another 3 to 4 minutes on the other side, covered.

Take the lid off and top the chicken with some of the browned onions at this stage. Put the drained rice on top of the chicken and onions. Add the 2½ cups (600 ml) of water and the remaining tablespoon (15 g) of ghee to the pot. Cover and cook for 20 minutes.

Open the lid and pour in the rose water, kewra water and saffron milk. Don't mix the rice once you've added these aromatics. This will ensure that you get some grains of rice that are white and some that are beautifully golden from the saffron. Spread the rest of the fried onions on top of the rice.

To help better retain the aromas, put some foil on the pot and then add the lid. Change the mode to Warm and let it sit in the pot for at least 10 minutes. Turn off the cooker and keep the lid on. Serve it after another 10 minutes. Garnish with coriander and lemon slices.

NOTE: *Kewra water is a floral extract derived from pandan leaves and a few drops bring a lot of fragrance to spiced rice dishes and lassis. You can find it in Indian supermarkets.*

PASTAS AND NOODLES

Anyone that knows me or my blog will be aware of my profound love for carbs—especially in the form of noodles and pasta. There is something so satisfying about slurping down a bowl of chewy, springy noodles or biting into pillowy, soft gnocchi. I also love the variety of shapes and sizes pasta comes in, like spiral fusilli, cylindrical rigatoni and farfalle, which resemble the cutest bow ties!

The rice cooker is a surprisingly good vessel to make pasta. In this chapter, you will find everything from easy, stress-free dinner dishes like Tuscan Tomato Penne (page 40), to more elaborate noodle soups like my Punchy Thai Red Curry Noodles (page 52) or handmade pastas like Gnudi with Sage Butter (Italian Ricotta Dumplings) (page 55), for when you really want to impress your guests. But regardless of the effort involved, they are all absolutely delicious crowd-pleasers.

LUSCIOUS SWEET CORN ALFREDO FARFALLE

Alfredo is the most indulgent of pasta sauces, in my opinion, being a thick blend of butter, cream and Parmesan. But if you'd like to try a vegan or slightly less caloric version of the dish, you'll be pleased to know that blended sweet corn can give you a very similar silky, rich texture and that luxurious taste, while feeling light and summery! It's also so beautiful and golden! In this recipe, I used farfalle pasta, but you can use any shorter or coiled pasta varieties that are easy to fit into and cook in the rice cooker pot.

Yield: 3–4 servings

For the Sweet Corn Cream Sauce

1 tbsp (14 g) unsalted butter

2 tbsp (20 g) chopped white onions

2 cups (320 g) canned sweet corn, drained

2 tsp (5 g) minced garlic

1 cup (240 ml) water

1 tbsp (15 ml) extra virgin olive oil

1 tbsp (15 ml) lemon juice

1 tbsp (15 ml) honey

Pinch of salt

For the Pasta

Salt, for boiling water, plus more to taste

12 oz (340 g) farfalle

2 tbsp (28 g) unsalted butter

½ cup (80 g) finely diced red onions

½ cup (80 g) canned sweet corn, drained

1 tsp minced garlic

¾ cup (180 ml) light cream

1 tbsp (2 g) finely chopped parsley

½ cup (50 g) grated Parmesan

Freshly ground black pepper, to taste

½ tsp chili flakes, to serve

To prepare the sweet corn cream sauce, turn on the rice cooker, set the mode to Cook and add the lid to let the rice cooker preheat for about 1 minute. Add the butter to the rice cooker pot. Put on the lid and let the butter melt, which will take 1 to 2 minutes. Then add the white onions and fry them for 3 to 4 minutes with the lid on. Add the corn and cook for another 4 to 5 minutes with the lid on. Toss in the garlic and sauté it for 1 to 2 minutes, or until it is fragrant. Turn off the cooker. Remove the contents of the rice cooker to a blender and add the water, olive oil, lemon juice, honey and salt. Blend until it's smooth. Set it aside.

To begin the pasta, clean out the rice cooker pot and add 3 cups (720 ml) of water and some salt. Cover and cook for 8 to 10 minutes. When the water boils, lift up the rice cooker lid and add the farfalle. Stir the pasta gently to prevent it from sticking to the base of the pot. Cover the rice cooker and allow the pasta to cook for about 10 minutes, until al dente or done to your taste. Turn off the rice cooker. Drain the pasta, reserving about ½ cup (120 ml) of pasta water and set it aside.

Dry the rice cooker pot fully. Turn on the rice cooker, set the mode to Cook and add the lid to let the rice cooker preheat for about 1 minute. Add the butter to the pot and put the lid back on. Cook for 1 to 2 minutes, or until the butter melts. Then add the red onions and fry them with the lid on for 3 to 4 minutes, or until they start to become golden brown. Now add the sweet corn and fry everything for 4 to 5 minutes more.

The garlic goes in at this stage. Sauté for another minute before adding the sweet corn sauce. Mix it all together and fry it for 2 to 3 minutes before adding the drained pasta. Thin out the sauce with some reserved pasta water if needed. Now add the cream and parsley and mix well.

Turn the rice cooker mode to Warm and then add in the Parmesan. Toss it well and season with salt and pepper. Finish with a sprinkle of red chili flakes.

TRUFFLE MUSHROOM MAC AND CHEESE

Mac and cheese doesn't get any more gourmet than this! Truffle oil elevates this easy pasta dish to the next level. It's the perfect dish to jazz up midweek meals, making for an excellent entrée and working equally well as a starter or a side with a juicy steak. You can top it with some toasted panko crumbs for added texture, but I like to serve it as is and let that glossy, cheesy sauce be the hero!

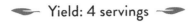 Yield: 4 servings

2 tbsp (28 g) unsalted butter, divided

1 cup (75 g) sliced mushrooms

Salt and freshly ground black pepper, to taste

2½ cups (600 ml) whole milk

2 cups (400 g) macaroni

1 cup (100 g) grated sharp cheddar cheese

1 cup (100 g) grated mild cheddar cheese

1 tbsp (8 g) cornstarch or corn flour

1 tbsp (15 ml) truffle oil, to serve

1 tsp chives, to serve

Turn on the rice cooker, set the mode to Cook and add the lid to let the rice cooker preheat for about 1 minute. Add in 1 tablespoon (14 g) of butter and close the lid. Let the butter melt, which should take 1 to 2 minutes. Once the butter melts, add the mushrooms and season them with salt and pepper. Add the lid and cook for 7 to 8 minutes, or until the mushrooms are softened, stirring midway through. Set them aside.

Now add the milk to the rice cooker along with the remaining 1 tablespoon (14 g) of butter, cover and cook for 6 to 7 minutes, or until the milk comes to a gentle boil. When the milk boils, lift up the rice cooker lid, add the macaroni pasta and then cover the rice cooker again. Allow the pasta to cook for 5 to 6 minutes.

While the pasta is cooking, in a small bowl, mix the sharp and mild cheddar cheeses. Sprinkle the cornstarch or corn flour over it, then stir the mixture to coat the cheese strands nicely. Remove the cooker lid and add the cheeses to the macaroni. Cook, covered, for another 5 to 6 minutes, or until the pasta is al dente. Then add the fried mushrooms back into the pot and give it all a good mix.

Serve it with a drizzle of truffle oil and a sprinkle of chives.

TUSCAN TOMATO PENNE

Sun-dried tomatoes have been used in Italian cuisine for centuries. Apparently, the Italian technique of adding salt to tomatoes and then drying them on rooftops might date as far back as 700 A.D. Sun-dried tomatoes give the dish a strong sweetness with a hint of tart, which helps balance the cream added to the sauce, making this Tuscan pasta luscious, creamy and scrumptious. This one-pot pasta is perfect for cooking in a rice cooker—there is no need to separately cook and drain the penne. You just prepare the luscious, garlicky sun-dried tomato sauce and simmer the pasta in it until it's al dente.

 Yield: 2 servings

2 tbsp (28 g) unsalted butter

½ cup (80 g) minced red onions

2 tbsp plus 1 tsp (20 g) minced garlic

4 oz (115 g) sun-dried tomatoes, drained and chopped

¼ tsp paprika

¼ tsp red chili flakes, plus more to serve

½ tsp Italian seasoning

Salt, to taste

1 cup (240 ml) whole milk

1 cup (240 ml) vegetable stock

8 oz (225 g) penne pasta

½ cup (120 ml) light cream

2 tsp (4 g) freshly grated Parmesan

1 tbsp (3 g) chopped fresh basil, to serve

Turn on the rice cooker, set the mode to Cook and add the lid to let the rice cooker preheat for about 1 minute.

Add the butter to the rice cooker and put the lid back on. The butter will take 1 to 2 minutes to melt. When melted, toss in the onions, garlic and sun-dried tomatoes. Sauté them for 2 minutes, then put the lid on and cook them for another 4 to 5 minutes, or until the onions are softened. Sprinkle in the paprika, red chili flakes, Italian seasoning and salt and fry for 1 to 2 minutes more, or until fragrant.

Now pour in the milk and stock, scraping up all the tasty brown bits at the bottom of the pot. Add the pasta and put the lid on. Cook it for 8 to 10 minutes, or until the pasta is al dente. Stir it every 2 to 3 minutes to make sure it doesn't stick to the bottom of the pot. If the sauce seems to be getting too thick, you can pour in a few more ladles of water to thin it out.

Change the rice cooker mode to Warm. Add the cream and stir it in. Sprinkle in the Parmesan and mix it into the dish. Serve it with fresh basil and more salt and chili flakes if desired.

COZY CHICKEN BUN GA (VIETNAMESE NOODLE SOUP)

Bun ga is the lighter, clearer version of pho. This Vietnamese noodle soup features shredded chicken, bean sprouts and aromatic herbs in a beautifully balanced and flavorsome broth. I highly recommend getting ahold of Kaffir lime leaves for this dish. They can be found in the fresh or frozen section of most Asian stores and just a few thin pieces can significantly elevate the aroma of this soup. To help you get a really clear soup, you can either parboil the chicken with white wine vinegar and salt or rub the chicken with salt and white wine and then rinse it well before use.

 Yield: 2 servings

For the Noodles

4 cups (960 ml) chicken stock

4 cloves garlic, crushed

1 tbsp (7 g) finely chopped fresh ginger

4 cloves

2 star anise

1 cinnamon stick

2 cardamom pods

2 tbsp (30 ml) lime juice

2 tbsp (2 g) fresh coriander

2 tbsp (2 g) fresh basil

1 red chili, sliced

9 oz (255 g) chicken breast

⅔ cup (80 g) apple, peeled and cut up into chunks

1 tbsp (15 ml) fish sauce

1 tsp granulated sugar

3 oz (85 g) bean sprouts

3½ oz (100 g) rice vermicelli noodles

For the Toppings

Fresh herbs (mint, cilantro, basil)

Lime wedges

Bean sprouts

Chilies

Radish slices

Place the stock, garlic, ginger, cloves, star anise, cinnamon stick, cardamom, lime juice, coriander, basil and red chili into the rice cooker pot. Cover and set the rice cooker to Cook for 8 to 10 minutes, or until the whole spices are fragrant and the broth comes to a boil.

Add the chicken to the pot, put the lid back on and cook it for 5 to 6 minutes, or until the chicken is done. Then remove the lid, take out the chicken and set it aside.

At this stage, add the apple chunks, fish sauce and sugar. Cook them with the lid on for 3 to 4 minutes more. Remove the whole spices now and add the bean sprouts, noodles and chicken back into the broth. Cover and cook for 4 to 5 minutes, or until the noodles are done.

Take out the chicken and shred it. Add the noodles and shredded chicken to the bowls and then ladle in the broth. Top with your herbs of choice, lime wedges, bean sprouts, chilies and radish.

SILKY LEEK AND ROQUEFORT ORZO

This orzo dish is pure comfort—the Roquefort makes it creamy, tangy and just sublime with the silky soft leeks. Mini rice-shaped orzo absorbs liquid and flavor just like rice, yet unlike traditional risotto, it's a lot easier to achieve a perfectly al dente creamy result without constant stirring. While it's perfect as is, feel free to top it with some crispy bacon for your meat-loving friends!

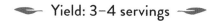 Yield: 3–4 servings

2 cups (300 g) finely sliced leeks

1 tbsp (14 g) unsalted butter

1 tbsp (15 ml) olive oil

½ cup (80 g) finely chopped white onions

Pinch of salt

¾ cup (160 g) orzo

1 cup (240 ml) dry white wine

2 cups (480 ml) chicken stock

1 tbsp (4 g) finely chopped fresh parsley

3 oz (85 g) Roquefort cheese, crumbled, plus more to serve

1 tbsp (15 ml) lemon juice

2–3 walnuts, chopped, divided

Begin by soaking the leeks in a pot of boiling water for 3 to 4 minutes. Strain them and set them aside.

Turn on the rice cooker, set the mode to Cook and add the lid to let the rice cooker preheat for about 1 minute.

Add the butter and olive oil to the pot when it's heated. Cover it and let the butter melt for 1 to 2 minutes, then toss in the onions. Season with salt and sauté the onions for a minute before putting the lid on and cooking them for 4 to 5 minutes, or until they are golden.

Now add the leeks, sauté for 2 minutes and then put on the lid, frying them until they are softened. This should take another 4 to 5 minutes.

Add in the orzo and stir well. Pour in the wine and stir everything together. Cook, covered, for 8 to 10 minutes. Give everything another stir and add in the stock. Cook for another 7 to 10 minutes, or until the orzo is fully cooked.

Change the cooker mode to Warm. Add the parsley, Roquefort, lemon juice and most of the walnuts. Mix well and serve with a sprinkle of the remaining walnuts and some more of the crumbled, creamy Roquefort.

EARTHY TAHINI NOODLE BOWL

These tahini noodles are my take on one of my all-time favorites: Sichuan Dan Dan noodles. They are delicious served both hot and cold. I'm using fettuccine because I feel that the wider noodle strands offer more surface area for the creamy sesame dressing to coat but it works equally great with ramen noodles, rice noodles or even spaghetti. The sauce is a garlicky, nutty blend of tahini, sesame oil, agave and soy sauce, which is surprisingly addictive.

If I had to stick to cooking the same noodle dish for the rest of my life, I think this would be it, which goes to show just how much I love it. I cannot wait for you to try it, too!

Yield: 4 servings

For the Sauce

½ cup (120 ml) reduced-sodium soy sauce

½ cup (120 ml) tahini

1 tbsp (7 g) grated fresh ginger

2 tbsp (17 g) minced garlic

3 tbsp (45 ml) agave syrup

2 tbsp (30 ml) toasted sesame oil

2 tbsp (30 ml) unseasoned rice wine vinegar

1 tbsp (15 ml) sriracha

1 tsp freshly ground black pepper

For the Noodles

1 lb (450 g) fettuccine

Salt, to taste

1 tbsp (15 ml) vegetable oil

½ cup (80 g) diced red onions

7 oz (200 g) zucchini, diced

7 oz (200 g) mushrooms, sliced

2 tsp (5 g) sesame seeds, to serve

1 tbsp (3 g) finely sliced scallions, to serve

Let's start off by making the sauce. In a blender, add the soy sauce, tahini, ginger, garlic, agave syrup, sesame oil, rice wine vinegar, sriracha and pepper and blend until smooth. Set the sauce aside.

For the noodles, add 3 cups (720 ml) of water to the rice cooker, cover and set to Cook. When the water boils, which will take 8 to 10 minutes, lift up the rice cooker lid and add the fettuccine pasta. Season generously with salt and stir the pasta gently to prevent it from sticking to the base of the pot. Cover the rice cooker and allow the pasta to cook for about 7 minutes, until al dente or done to your taste. Drain and set it aside.

Dry the rice cooker completely. Turn on the rice cooker, set the mode to Cook and add the lid to let the rice cooker preheat for about 1 minute.

Add the vegetable oil to the pot, put the lid back on and let it heat up for 1 to 2 minutes. Once the oil has heated up, toss in the onions and sauté them for a minute. Put the lid on and fry them for 4 to 5 minutes more, or until they're softened.

Now add the zucchini and mushrooms, sautéing for 1 to 2 minutes. Then cover and cook for 5 to 7 minutes, or until the mushrooms are browned. Finally, add the drained fettuccine and pour over the sauce. Toss it well and serve it with a sprinkle of sesame seeds and scallions.

SPICY TTEOKBOKKI (KOREAN RICE CAKES)

When I was in Seoul, this was the one dish I spotted in every street food market in town. Tteokbokki is made with cylindrical, chewy rice cakes tossed in a spicy, umami-rich sauce. I tried many different versions of the dish in Seoul, like curry tteokbokki, seafood tteokbokki and even tteokbokki pizza! But I will stick to the traditional recipe for today. You will notice that the recipe requires Korean soup stock but if you can't find it, just use water or make your own stock by soaking dried anchovies in water for 20 minutes and then boiling them in the water for 10 to 12 minutes. Then strain out the anchovies and use the stock! You could also flavor it by adding radish, garlic or spring onions with the anchovies which will all act as wonderful aromatics!

← Yield: 2 servings →

For the Sauce

3 tbsp (24 g) gochujang (Korean chili paste)

3 tbsp (45 g) granulated sugar

1 tbsp (15 ml) soy sauce, or to taste

1 tbsp (9 g) minced garlic

1 tsp gochugaru (Korean chili flakes)

For the Rice Cakes

12 oz (340 g) Korean rice cakes, separated

3 cups (720 ml) Korean soup stock or water

4 oz (115 g) Korean fish cakes, rinsed with hot water and cut into bite-sized pieces

⅓ cup (55 g) thinly sliced white onions

1 tsp roasted sesame seeds, to serve

1 stalk spring onions, finely chopped, to serve

1 tsp sesame oil, to serve

For the sauce, in a small bowl, mix the gochujang, sugar, soy sauce, garlic and gochugaru and set it aside.

In a bowl of warm water, soak the rice cakes for 10 minutes to soften them. In the meantime, turn on the rice cooker and pour the soup stock or water into the pot. Set the rice cooker to Cook and put the lid on. Bring the stock to a boil, which will take 10 to 12 minutes. Midway through, remove the lid to add in the sauce, stirring it in until it fully dissolves.

For the rice cake portion of the dish, add the rice cakes, fish cakes and onions to the stock. Cover and cook them for another 4 to 5 minutes, or until the rice cakes are soft and tender. Change the cooker mode to Warm and simmer for 2 to 3 minutes more to thicken the sauce.

Garnish the dish with the roasted sesame seeds and spring onions and drizzle with sesame oil before serving.

INDULGENT GNOCCHI CACIO E PEPE

What's not to like about these soft, pillowy Italian dumplings? Baked, boiled or fried—gnocchi are great every way. Here I am serving them in the cacio e pepe style, which is perhaps my favorite pasta sauce of all time. It uses only two main ingredients: black pepper and pecorino cheese. Cacio e pepe is a classic Roman dish—Italians would just combine the cheese and pepper with spaghetti water, but I do cheat by adding a bit of butter to help bring the sauce together.

≈ Yield: 2–3 servings ≈

For the Gnocchi

1 lb (450 g) floury potatoes (I would suggest Maris Piper or Russet)

¾ cup (100 g) all-purpose flour or '00' flour, plus more as needed

2 tsp (12 g) salt, plus more for boiling the pasta

For the Sauce

3 tbsp (42 g) unsalted butter

⅔ cup (60 g) grated pecorino or Parmesan, plus some more to serve

2 tsp (4 g) freshly ground black pepper

Salt, to taste

To make the gnocchi, add the potatoes to the rice cooker. Pour in just enough water so the potatoes are fully submerged. Put on the lid and set the rice cooker to Cook. Let the potatoes cook for 25 to 30 minutes, or until they are tender.

Drain the potatoes, then set them aside until they are cool enough to handle. Once they have cooled down, peel and mash them in a bowl. Add the flour and salt. Mix it all together until a dough starts to form. Feel free to add some more flour if the dough feels too wet. Make sure to only add a bit of flour at a time and judge if any more is needed.

Lightly flour a work surface. Knead this dough on the floured surface for a few minutes until it's pliable. Portion it into four equal pieces and roll each piece into a log that's about 1 inch (2.5 cm) in diameter. Slice up the log into 1-inch (2.5-cm) pieces, which you can roll into balls, or roll over the back of a grater or fork, to give it grooves, which can help the sauce stick better.

Next, add 4 cups (960 ml) of water and a generous amount of salt to the rice cooker, put on the lid and set it to Cook. Let the water come to a boil, which will take 12 to 15 minutes. Add the gnocchi to the boiling water and cook them for 2 to 3 minutes. It's easiest to do it in two batches so they are less likely to break. Save about ½ cup (120 ml) of the pasta water and drain out the rest. Set the gnocchi aside.

To make the sauce, after drying out the rice cooker, turn it on to Cook and add the lid to preheat the rice cooker for about 1 minute.

Add the butter, cover and give the butter 1 to 2 minutes to melt. Once it begins to melt, add the pecorino cheese and the pepper. Pour in 2 tablespoons (30 ml) of the pasta water and mix it all together, creating our smooth pasta sauce. If it feels too thick, add in 2 to 3 tablespoons (30 to 45 ml) more of the pasta water. Season with salt.

Toss in the gnocchi and coat it well in the sauce. Serve it with some more freshly grated pecorino.

PUNCHY THAI RED CURRY NOODLES

Curries traditionally tend to be served with rice but I'm a big fan of serving them with noodles—what's not to like about slurping on a luscious curry broth as you bite into chewy noodles, all from one big, steaming bowl of deliciousness? The spicy chilies, umami shrimp paste and creamy coconut milk in this curry combine to give you a flavor-packed yet balanced broth, perfect with noodles. I'm making my own curry paste for a fresher, more intense flavor but if you're in a rush, store-bought paste will work just fine. Either way, this is guaranteed to be a comforting, fragrant, heartwarming bowl of noodles which you'll definitely want to make again!

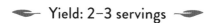 Yield: 2–3 servings

For the Thai Red Curry Paste

¼ cup (40 g) coarsely chopped red onions

3 tbsp (20 g) minced lemongrass

1 tsp red chili powder

2½ tbsp (27 g) minced garlic

1 oz (30 g) galangal or ginger, peeled and sliced

2 tbsp (30 ml) ketchup

2 tbsp (30 ml) fish sauce

2 tbsp (30 ml) lime juice

2 tsp (3 g) chili powder

4 tbsp (60 ml) coconut milk

1 tsp shrimp paste

1 tsp granulated sugar

1 tsp ground cumin

1 tsp ground coriander

½ tsp ground white pepper

½ tsp ground cinnamon

1–2 tsp (5–10 ml) water (optional)

To make the Thai red curry paste, in a blender, add the red onions, lemongrass, red chili powder, garlic, ginger, ketchup, fish sauce, lime juice, chili powder, coconut milk, shrimp paste, sugar, cumin, coriander, white pepper and cinnamon and blend until a smooth paste forms. Feel free to add 1 to 2 teaspoons (5 to 10 ml) of water to help with the blending, if needed. Set the paste aside. We will be using about 3 to 4 spoonfuls of it for the noodle soup, but you can store any of the leftover paste in an airtight container in the fridge for about 7 to 10 days.

(continued)

For the Noodles

4 oz (115 g) sweet potatoes, cubed

3½ oz (100 g) broccolini

2 tbsp (30 ml) olive oil

¼ cup (40 g) finely diced red onions

2 tbsp plus 1 tsp (20 g) minced garlic

1 tbsp (7 g) grated galangal or fresh ginger

1 tbsp (6 g) finely chopped lemongrass

3 tbsp (45 ml) Thai Red Curry Paste, previously made

1 cup (240 ml) coconut milk

1½ cups (360 ml) chicken stock

4 oz (115 g) rice noodles

3½ oz (100 g) baby corn

1 tbsp (15 ml) fish sauce

2 tsp (10 g) brown sugar

Salt, to taste

2 Kaffir lime leaves

1 tbsp (2 g) chopped cilantro, to serve

1 tbsp (3 g) thinly sliced scallions, to serve

To begin the noodles, add 3 cups (720 ml) of water to the rice cooker. Put the lid on and set the rice cooker to Cook for 10 to 12 minutes. Once the water comes to a boil, place the cubed sweet potatoes in the steamer basket and position the basket above the water in the rice cooker. Steam the potatoes, covered, for 12 minutes, and then remove the lid. Add the broccolini to the steamer basket and pop the lid back on. Steam for another 2 to 3 minutes, or until the vegetables are tender. Set them aside and then dry out the rice cooker pot completely.

Next, turn on the rice cooker, set the mode to Cook and add the lid to let the rice cooker preheat for about 1 minute. Add the olive oil, cover and let the oil heat up for 1 to 2 minutes. Once the oil has heated up, add in the onions and sauté them for a minute. Then add the lid and let them fry for 5 to 6 minutes more, or until they are translucent, stirring frequently. Now add the garlic, galangal and lemongrass. Sauté them for a minute and then cook for 3 to 4 minutes with the lid on. If the mix seems too dry, stir in a small splash of water.

Now add the Thai red curry paste and sauté everything for 2 minutes. Cover and cook for 2 to 3 more minutes, or until you see the oils separating. Stir in the coconut milk and stock, scraping off any brown bits at the bottom. Cover and cook for 7 to 8 minutes, or until the soup has reduced. Then add the rice noodles, steamed sweet potato and broccolini, baby corn, fish sauce and brown sugar. Cook, with the lid on, for a further 5 to 6 minutes, or until the noodles are tender.

Season with salt and stir in the Kaffir lime leaves. Serve with the cilantro and scallions.

GNUDI WITH SAGE BUTTER (ITALIAN RICOTTA DUMPLINGS)

Gnudi is one of Tuscany's best kept secrets. I say it's a secret as I have hardly ever seen a restaurant in London, or anywhere else outside Italy, serve it! Yet it's so simple, so comforting and probably one of the quickest fresh pastas to make. Think of gnudi as the fluffier, cheesier siblings of gnocchi. While gnocchi tends to be made with a starchy base of potatoes and flour, gnudi are made with fresh ricotta. Interestingly, the term "gnudi" in the Tuscan dialect means "naked," as it is seen as a naked version of ravioli, since the combination of ingredients used to make these dumplings is similar to what you'd see inside a ravioli.

 Yield: 4 servings

14 oz (400 g) fresh spinach

⅔ cup (150 g) unsalted butter, divided

14 oz (400 g) ricotta cheese

2 small eggs

6 oz (170 g) grated Parmesan, plus more to serve

6 oz (170 g) all-purpose flour, plus more for flouring tray

Salt, to taste

Freshly ground black pepper, to taste

½ tsp grated nutmeg

Add 2 cups (480 ml) of water to the rice cooker pot and set it to Cook. Let it heat up for 8 to 10 minutes with the lid closed until the water comes to a boil. After removing the spinach stalks, wash the leaves properly and place them in the steamer basket. Fit the steamer basket in its place in the rice cooker and close the lid. Cook for 10 to 20 minutes, or until the spinach is soft and wilted. Alternatively, just pour boiling water over the spinach for 30 seconds to 1 minute, then drain and set the leaves aside.

Once the spinach is cool enough to handle, squeeze out the water. Chop it into smaller pieces with a knife or a pair of kitchen scissors. We want to avoid blending it, so it retains some of its texture.

Turn on the rice cooker, set the mode to Cook and add the lid to let the rice cooker preheat for about 1 minute. Add 2 tablespoons (28 g) of butter to the rice cooker pot. Cover and let the butter melt for 1 to 2 minutes. Once the butter melts, add the spinach and fry it for 2 to 3 minutes. This will enhance its flavor and help dry it out further, which in turn will help bring together the mixture for the gnudi. Remove the spinach to a bowl and set it aside.

Once the spinach has slightly cooled, add in the ricotta and stir together with a fork until you get a cohesive mix. Now add the eggs and grated Parmesan. Mix well and then sift in the flour, little by little, continuing to stir. You should have a mixture that is soft but pliable. Season with salt and pepper and add the nutmeg.

(continued)

GNUDI WITH SAGE BUTTER
(ITALIAN RICOTTA DUMPLINGS) (CONT.)

½ cup (84 g) semolina, to use during shaping

8–10 sage leaves

Put the semolina in a small bowl. Use a spoon to scoop out some of the gnudi mix and then roll it into a ball. Roll it around in the bowl of semolina to coat it nicely and then pick it up and roll it further with your hands until you have a smooth ball. Put the shaped gnudi on a floured tray. Repeat this until you have the remaining gnudi prepared. Place the tray in the fridge for at least an hour to help them set.

About 10 minutes before bringing them out of the fridge, heat up salted water in the rice cooker. For this, turn on the rice cooker and add in 4 cups (960 ml) of water. Season well with salt. Close the lid and set the cooker to Cook. The water will take 12 to 15 minutes to come to a boil. Then add the gnudi to the water for 4 to 5 minutes, or until they float to the surface. Remove them and put them in your serving dish. It might be easier to cook the gnudi in two batches depending on how much space you have in the rice cooker.

Once the gnudi are prepared, dry out the rice cooker pot completely. Turn on the rice cooker, set the mode to Cook and add the lid to let the rice cooker preheat for about 1 minute.

Add the remaining 8½ tablespoons (122 g) of the butter to the pot. Set the cooker to Cook, put the lid on and let the butter melt for 1 to 2 minutes.

Fry the sage leaves in the melted butter for 2 to 3 minutes, or until the sage is fragrant. Then add the gnudi and toss them in the melted butter. Fry them for 1 to 2 minutes, until they are lightly golden, then plate them. Serve them with some grated Parmesan.

SAUCY YAKI UDON (JAPANESE STIR-FRIED NOODLES)

Yaki udon is a popular Japanese stir-fried udon noodle dish. This is one of my go-to lunch recipes and it's honestly such a great way to use up your leftover fridge stash. I love udon noodles because they are so thick and chewy. For this recipe, I use pre-cooked udon noodles that you typically find in vacuum-packed plastic cases in the refrigerated or frozen section of most Asian grocery stores. However, you can use dried or fresh udon noodles. Cook them according to the package instructions but for 1 to 2 minutes less to allow for the additional cooking that'll take place when you stir-fry the noodles.

Yield: 3–4 servings

For the Sauce

2½ tbsp (37 ml) dark soy sauce

1 tbsp (15 ml) oyster sauce

2 tbsp (30 ml) mirin

2 tsp (10 g) brown sugar

1 tbsp (15 ml) sesame oil

2 tsp (5 g) minced garlic

For the Noodles

1 tbsp (15 ml) vegetable oil

½ tbsp (8 ml) sesame oil

1 oz (30 g) mushrooms, thinly sliced

⅓ cup (30 g) broccoli, cut up into florets

¼ cup (40 g) sliced bell peppers

⅔ cup (50 g) shredded cabbage

⅓ cup (40 g) grated carrots

1 oz (30 g) scallions, green stalks cut into 2-inch (5-cm) pieces (save the whites for another recipe)

12 oz (340 g) pre-cooked udon noodles

Sesame seeds, to serve

For the sauce, in a small bowl, mix together the soy sauce, oyster sauce, mirin, brown sugar, sesame oil and garlic. Set it aside.

To begin the noodle portion of the dish, turn on the rice cooker, set the mode to Cook and add the lid to let the rice cooker preheat for about 1 minute. Pour in the vegetable oil and sesame oil and add the lid. Let the oils heat up for 1 to 2 minutes. Once the oil mix is heated, add the mushrooms and sauté them for a minute. Close the lid and cook them for 3 to 4 minutes, or until they're lightly golden. Then add the broccoli and fry for 2 to 3 minutes. At this stage, toss in the bell peppers, cabbage, carrots and scallion greens. Sauté everything for a minute before adding the lid and cooking for another 2 to 3 minutes.

While you sauté the vegetables, prepare the noodles as per packet instructions. I am using pre-cooked ones which I simply transfer to a sieve, untangle under running water and then drain. Add the udon to the rice cooker pot along with the sauce and toss well. Stir-fry for 2 to 3 minutes more, or until everything is well combined. Serve the dish with a sprinkle of sesame seeds.

MEATY MAINS

This chapter of my book is dedicated to all you carnivores out there! Whether you're looking for an exciting midweek meal to feed the family or for a showstopping centerpiece for your dinner guests, the recipes in this chapter will sort you out.

A rice cooker is actually fantastic for cooking these dishes because you can slow-cook stews and curries in it and it is great for locking in the moisture, giving you tender, juicy meat each time. Since the rice cooker can't cook dishes on high heat, my only suggestion would be to make sure to lightly fry the meat as an initial step or to use minced or thinly-sliced meat where possible. This will make sure it cooks thoroughly. Also, I have used bone-in chicken and lamb pieces where possible to lend a deeper, richer flavor to the dishes. Bone-in pieces will also be less likely to dry out, which is essential, given that a lot of these recipes require slow cooking over a long time.

For those who like their spice, the Malaysian Curry Chicken (page 62) and the Bengali Lamb Curry (page 72) are must-try dishes. They are some of my all-time favorite curries because of the amount of flavor they pack in. Or, if you are after something that's more family-friendly, go for the Japanese Cream Pork Stew (page 65) or the hearty Rustic Chicken Cacciatore (page 68). They are filling, delicious dishes, which are bound to be a hit with kids and adults alike.

MALAYSIAN CURRY CHICKEN

Curry chicken is Malaysia's national dish with good reason. It is simple to make, yet utterly flavorful and satisfying. You'll find it on menus all over the country and it goes well with white rice or some buttery roti. It's a rich curry that's not too spicy but very aromatic from the use of lemongrass and curry leaves. I recommend letting the chicken curry rest for at least 30 minutes after cooking, which will help give the taste a more rounded flavor.

 Yield: 2 servings

For the Malaysian Curry Powder

2 tbsp (10 g) coriander seeds

1 tbsp (6 g) cumin seeds

½ tbsp (3 g) fennel seeds

½ tbsp (3 g) chili powder, to taste

½ tsp turmeric powder

¼ tsp cloves

¼ tsp cinnamon powder

2–3 cardamom pods

½ tsp whole black peppercorns

For the Curry

1 lb (450 g) chicken breasts and thighs

4 tbsp (24 g) Malaysian Curry Powder, previously prepared, divided

1 tbsp (15 ml) light soy sauce

2 tbsp (20 g) macadamia nuts, chopped

1 tbsp (9 g) minced garlic

1 cup (160 g) chopped red onions

2 tsp (4 g) grated fresh ginger

3–5 dried red chilies, soaked in water for 30 minutes

3 tbsp (45 ml) vegetable oil, divided

To make the curry powder, in a grinder place the coriander seeds, cumin seeds, fennel seeds, chili powder, turmeric powder, cloves, cinnamon, cardamom pods and peppercorns and blend them, then set the powder aside.

In a large bowl, marinate the chicken meat with 2 teaspoons (6 g) of the Malaysian curry powder and the soy sauce for at least 30 minutes.

In the grinder, blend the macadamia nuts, garlic, red onions, ginger and dried chilies with the remaining curry powder. Add 1 to 2 teaspoons (5 to 10 ml) of the vegetable oil if the mix seems too dry. Set it aside.

(continued)

MALAYSIAN CURRY CHICKEN (CONT.)

⅔ cup (110 g) sliced yellow onions

10 oz (285 g) Yukon Gold or other medium-starch potatoes, cut into large chunks

1 lemongrass stalk

5 curry leaves

1 cup (240 ml) coconut milk

Salt and granulated sugar

Lemon wedges and red chili slices, to serve

To begin the curry, turn on the rice cooker, set the mode to Cook and add the lid to let the rice cooker preheat for about 1 minute. Pour the remaining oil—2 tablespoons (30 ml) plus 1 to 2 teaspoons (5 to 10 ml)—into the rice cooker pot. Put on the lid. Give the oil 1 to 2 minutes to heat up. Lift the lid and add in the onions. Sauté them for a minute and then fry them, covered, for 3 to 4 minutes, or until they're translucent. Now add the blended paste you made in the previous paragraph and fry with the onions for 2 to 3 minutes, or until it's fragrant.

Then add in the chicken and toss well. Cover and cook the chicken for 2 minutes. Flip the pieces and cook them again, covered, for another 2 minutes. Pour in 2 cups (480 ml) of water. Cook with the lid on for another 4 to 5 minutes before adding the potatoes, lemongrass and curry leaves.

Cover and cook everything for another 20 to 25 minutes, or until the chicken is fully cooked.

Add in the coconut milk and stir it in well. Add some salt and sugar to taste—I generally add ½ to 2 teaspoons (3 to 10 g) of sugar, depending on how spicy I want the curry to be. Change the rice cooker mode to Warm. Simmer the curry with the lid on for another 3 to 4 minutes. Serve it hot with lemon wedges and sliced red chilies.

JAPANESE CREAM PORK STEW

Cream stew is a popular Japanese dish served at home and in local restaurants and cafés. In Japanese cuisine, this is a Yoshuku dish. This cuisine essentially involves Western dishes that have been reinvented and tailored to the Japanese palette. Yoshuku dates back to the Meiji era of the late nineteenth century, when Japan opened its borders and was firmly integrating Western elements in an effort to avoid being colonized by the Western powers, like their neighbors. Japanese cream stew, a.k.a. white stew, features a rich and creamy broth that is delicious yet not heavy. It is best served with white rice or a warm baguette.

 Yield: 4–6 servings

For the Roux

¾ cup (180 ml) heavy cream

5 tbsp (40 g) all-purpose flour

1 tbsp (8 g) milk powder

For the Stew

1 lb (450 g) pork shoulder, trimmed and cut into 1-inch (2.5-cm) pieces

Salt and freshly ground black pepper, to taste

1½ cups (120 g) broccoli, cut up into florets

2 tbsp (30 ml) vegetable oil

To make the roux, in a small bowl, stir together the heavy cream, flour and milk powder until you get a smooth paste and set it aside.

To start the stew, season the pork with salt and pepper and set it aside. Add 3 cups (720 ml) of water to the rice cooker and put the lid on. Set it to Cook and let the water come to a boil, which should take 7 to 8 minutes. During this time, add water and ice to a large bowl. Then add the broccoli to the boiling water, cover and cook it for 3 to 4 minutes. Remove the blanched broccoli to the bowl of ice water and set it aside.

Pour out the water and dry the rice cooker pot. Turn on the rice cooker, set the mode to Cook and add the lid to let the rice cooker preheat for about 1 minute.

Add the vegetable oil to the pot and put on the lid. Let the oil heat up for 1 to 2 minutes before adding the diced pork. Sauté the pork for a minute and then add the lid. Let it fry for 2 to 3 minutes, or until the pork starts to brown on one side. Flip the pieces over and fry them, covered, for another 1 to 2 minutes, or until the other side is lightly golden brown.

(continued)

JAPANESE CREAM PORK STEW (CONT.)

1 cup (160 g) chopped white onions

1 cup (130 g) diced carrots

2 cups (300 g) cubed Yukon Gold potatoes

3 cups (720 ml) vegetable stock

Salt, to taste

¼ tsp ground white pepper

1 bay leaf

2 tbsp (30 ml) heavy cream

1 tsp granulated sugar

Whole milk (optional)

All-purpose flour (optional)

Freshly ground black pepper, to taste

Now add in the onions. Fry them for 2 minutes more before adding the carrots and potatoes. Sauté them for a minute and then cover and cook for 5 to 6 minutes more, until the onions are translucent but not browned. At this stage, add the stock, salt, white pepper and bay leaf and mix well, removing any brown bits from the bottom and deglazing the pot. Cover and cook for 10 to 12 minutes, or until it comes to a gentle boil. Then add the blanched broccoli and cook for another 3 to 4 minutes, or until the potatoes are fully cooked.

Pour a few ladles of the stew into your roux and whisk to dissolve the roux until there are no lumps. Change the rice cooker mode to Warm. Then add the roux, cream and sugar into the pot.

Stir well and simmer for another 2 to 3 minutes. If the stew seems too thick, pour in some milk, or if it seems too thin, add a sprinkle of flour and stir it in. Remove the bay leaf before serving the stew with some freshly ground black pepper, if desired.

RUSTIC CHICKEN CACCIATORE

The term "cacciatore" means "hunter" in Italian. This is the type of dish that would be made by Italian hunters' wives for their husbands after they'd return from a hard day of toil in the countryside. There are many different variations of the dish, as is the case with most Italian classics, but it is essentially a casserole-style dish cooked in a tomato-based sauce and served frequently with pasta.

I am sticking to a more traditional version of the dish, but feel free to jazz it up with capers, anchovies, mushrooms, corn and any other toppings you want. Also, instead of pasta, you can choose to serve this dish with garlic bread, mashed swede, roasted potatoes or even lentils, for a healthier alternative.

 Yield: 2 servings

3 tbsp (45 ml) olive oil, divided

9 oz (255 g) chicken thighs

¼ cup (30 g) all-purpose flour mixed with a pinch of salt, for dusting

⅔ cup (110 g) finely chopped white onions

2 tbsp (17 g) crushed cloves garlic

1½ cups (225 g) sliced red peppers

¼ cup (60 ml) dry white wine

2 cups (360 g) chopped tomatoes

2 cups (480 ml) chicken stock

Salt, to taste

¼ cup (45 g) olives without pits, drained

2 tbsp (5 g) chopped fresh parsley, to serve

Turn on the rice cooker, set the mode to Cook and add the lid to let the rice cooker preheat for about 1 minute. Add 2 tablespoons (30 ml) of the olive oil to the rice cooker pot. Put the lid on and let it heat up for 1 to 2 minutes. While the oil is heating up, dust the chicken with the salted flour and then add it to the pot. Fry it for 3 to 4 minutes on each side, covered, until lightly browned. Remove the chicken and set it aside.

Add the remaining tablespoon (15 ml) of oil to the rice cooker pot and add the onions. Set the device to Cook. Sauté them for a minute, then put the lid on and fry the onions for 5 to 6 minutes, or until they are translucent. Now add the garlic and red peppers and fry for another 2 to 3 minutes.

Pour in the wine, add the lid back on and cook for 2 to 3 minutes, or until it comes to a simmer.

Throw in the tomatoes and stock, and return the chicken back to the pot. Stir well and season it with salt. Let the stew cook, covered, for 25 to 30 minutes, or until the chicken is fully cooked and tender.

Add the olives in at the end and sprinkle with parsley before serving.

RICH CHICKEN PAPRIKASH

This vibrant red dish is one of Hungary's most beloved. It features tender chicken cooked in a beautifully rich, creamy and flavorful sauce, infused with lots of paprika.

Hungarians tend to cook it in lard for an extra luxurious flavor, but ghee or butter will also work. Also, as the dish is centered around paprika, it is worth considering which type to use, as it will impact the flavor and intensity of the dish. There are two main types of paprika: Spanish and Hungarian. The main difference between these two types is that the former is made with smoked peppers instead of fresh, toasted peppers. It is better to use the Hungarian one for a more authentic taste in this recipe, but the Spanish one gives great results, too.

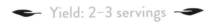 Yield: 2–3 servings

4 tbsp (56 g) lard or unsalted butter, divided

1½ lbs (680 g) chicken breast, bone-in and skin-on

1 cup (160 g) very finely chopped yellow onions

1 tbsp (9 g) finely minced garlic

14 oz (400 g) diced Roma tomatoes

Salt and freshly ground black pepper, to taste

3 tbsp (21 g) Hungarian paprika

1½ cups (360 ml) chicken broth

3 tbsp (25 g) all-purpose flour

½ cup (120 ml) sour cream

Fresh parsley, to serve

Turn on the rice cooker, set the mode to Cook and add the lid to let the rice cooker preheat for about 1 minute.

Add 3 tablespoons (42 g) of lard to the rice cooker. Put the lid on and let it heat up for 1 to 2 minutes. Place the chicken pieces in the pot and fry for a minute. Then add the lid. Cover and cook them for 3 to 4 minutes, or until the chicken is lightly browned on that side. Then remove the lid and flip them. Cook with the lid back on for another 2 to 3 minutes, or until they are browned on the other side. Remove the chicken pieces from the pot and set them aside.

Add the remaining tablespoon (14 g) of lard to the rice cooker. Add the lid and set it to Cook. Let it heat up for a minute and then toss in the onions. Sauté them for a minute and put the lid on. Cook them for 5 to 6 minutes, or until they're golden. Toss in the garlic and diced tomatoes. Fry them for 2 to 3 minutes. Season with salt, pepper and the paprika.

Fry the onion, garlic and tomato mixture for a few seconds before returning the chicken back to the pot. Coat it well in the sauce and then add in the broth. Close the lid and cook it for 25 to 30 minutes, or until the chicken is done.

In a small bowl, mix the flour with the sour cream, whisking until there are no lumps. Remove the chicken from the pot and keep it warm.

Stir the cream mixture into the sauce. Set the rice cooker mode to Warm, put the lid on and simmer the sauce for 2 to 3 minutes, until the sauce thickens. Adjust the amount of salt and pepper, if needed. Return the chicken to the sauce and let it warm through for 1 to 2 minutes before serving. Garnish it with fresh parsley.

BENGALI LAMB CURRY

If there's one dish from my childhood that I crave most, it is Bengali lamb curry, better known as "Kosha Mangsho." The word "kosha" comes from the Bengali word "koshano," which is a slow cooking technique that uses very little water, while the word "mangsho" refers to meat. So, the name translates to a slow-cooked, dry meat curry. It is a super-rich and delicious curry with a velvety, dark brown gravy and fatty, melt-in-your-mouth mutton.

Traditionally, the dish is made with goat meat but since mutton is hard to find in most other countries, including England, I am swapping it out for lamb, which has a very similar taste and flavor profile. I often serve it with luchi, a type of deep-fried bread popular in Bengali cuisine.

 Yield: 2–3 servings

1 lb (450 g) lamb, cut into 1-inch (2.5-cm) chunks

For the Marinade

2 tbsp (30 ml) plain Greek yogurt

1 tsp ginger paste

1 tsp garlic paste

1 tbsp (15 ml) mustard oil

For the Curry

4 tbsp (60 ml) mustard oil

2 bay leaves

2 cloves

3 green cardamom pods

2 whole black cardamom pods

1 cinnamon stick

½ tsp black peppercorns

4 whole dry red chilies

1 tsp granulated sugar

2 cups (320 g) chopped white onions

1 tbsp (9 g) garlic paste

1 tsp chopped green chilies

½ cup (90 g) chopped plum tomatoes

For the marinade, in a large bowl, mix the lamb with the yogurt, ginger paste, garlic paste and mustard oil. Add a lid to the bowl and refrigerate it for 4 to 5 hours.

For the curry, turn on the rice cooker, set the mode to Cook and add the lid to let the rice cooker preheat for about 1 minute. Add the mustard oil to the rice cooker pot. Cover and let it heat up for 1 to 2 minutes. Once the oil has heated up, add in the bay leaves. Lightly crush all the whole spices (cloves, green and black cardamom pods, cinnamon stick and peppercorns) and add them to the oil. Then add the dry red chilies and the sugar. Sauté everything for a few seconds.

Now add the onions, sauté them for a minute and put the lid on. Fry them, covered, for 5 to 6 minutes, or until they are a light brown. Then add in the garlic paste and green chilies and fry them, covered, for another 2 to 3 minutes, or until the onions are a darker brown. At this point, add in the tomatoes and fry them for 2 to 3 minutes, or until they turn darker.

(continued)

BENGALI LAMB CURRY (CONT.)

10 oz (285 g) medium Yukon Gold potatoes, peeled and cut into quarters

2 tsp (2 g) coriander powder

1 tsp turmeric powder

2 tsp (2 g) Kashmiri chili powder

1 tsp cumin powder

Salt, to taste

3 cups (720 ml) water

½ tsp garam masala

2 tbsp (30 g) ghee

1 tsp chopped coriander, to serve

Now add the marinated meat and the potatoes. Cover and cook the dish for 10 to 12 minutes.

Sprinkle in the coriander powder, turmeric powder, Kashmiri chili powder, cumin powder and salt, and fry everything for another 2 minutes, stirring well. Stir in 3 cups (720 ml) of water and cover the pan. Cook for 45 minutes to an hour, or until the lamb is tender.

Finally, add the garam masala and ghee and mix well. Set the rice cooker mode to Warm and let it stand for 8 to 10 minutes before serving it with the chopped coriander.

MUGHLAI KEEMA MATAR (GROUND LAMB AND PEA CURRY)

Keema matar is a scrumptious curry from the Northern part of India. "Keema" means ground meat and "matar" means peas. This dish, like many meat dishes from Northern India, is said to have Persian roots and was brought to India by the Mughals. Apparently, the royals would serve it for special occasions.

Growing up, I used to see my mum make this dish using mutton but, as it is a bit harder to source in England, I make mine with ground lamb—it's slightly less gamey and slightly more fatty than mutton, but it does work equally well. You may also add potatoes to this recipe, but make sure to add them in with the tomatoes to allow enough time for them to cook.

 Yield: 3–4 servings

1 lb (450 g) ground lamb

4 tbsp (60 ml) plain Greek yogurt

1 tsp salt, plus more to taste

½ cup (120 g) ghee, plus 1 tbsp (15 g) to serve

2 tsp (4 g) cumin seeds

1 tsp cloves

1 cinnamon stick

1 tsp whole peppercorns

½ tsp black cardamom seeds

2 bay leaves

1 tsp garlic paste

1 tsp ginger paste

1 cup (160 g) grated red onions

2 cups (360 g) chopped plum tomatoes

1 tbsp (5 g) coriander powder

½ tsp turmeric

½ tsp chili powder

In a large bowl, marinate the ground lamb in the yogurt and 1 teaspoon of salt. Let it sit for 30 minutes.

Turn on the rice cooker, set the mode to Cook and add the lid to let the rice cooker preheat for about 1 minute. Then add the ½ cup (120 g) of ghee, cover and let it melt for 1 to 2 minutes. Once the ghee melts, add the cumin seeds, cloves, cinnamon stick, peppercorns, cardamom seeds and bay leaves. Sauté them for a minute, then put the lid on and fry them for another 2 to 3 minutes, or until the seeds start to splutter.

Then add the garlic paste, ginger paste and onions, and fry them, covered, for 5 to 6 minutes, or until the onions are translucent. Now stir in the tomatoes, coriander powder, turmeric and chili powder. Season with salt. Stir-fry the dish for 2 to 3 minutes and then put on the lid. Cook it for another 3 to 4 minutes, or until the tomatoes are tender.

(continued)

MUGHLAI KEEMA MATAR
(GROUND LAMB AND PEA CURRY) (CONT.)

1 cup (140 g) canned green peas, drained

½ cup (120 ml) water

1 tsp garam masala, to serve

1 tbsp (1 g) chopped coriander leaves, to serve

Now add the marinated lamb and the peas. Fry them for 1 to 2 minutes, then add the water. Give it a good mix and then close the lid. Cook for 15 to 20 minutes, stirring midway through, until the lamb is fully cooked. If needed, adjust the seasoning at this stage.

Finish with a sprinkle of garam masala and 1 tablespoon (15 g) of ghee, and garnish with the chopped coriander leaves.

MOROCCAN CHICKEN TAGINE

A tagine is a slow-cooked stew combining sweet and savory elements, like dried fruits and harissa. When I was in Marrakesh, I had it every single day with a warm fluffy pita and a side of fresh mint tea—it was heaven!

The dish is the essence of Moroccan cuisine which is distinguished by its Arabic, Berber and French influences. The stew gets its name from the vessel it's traditionally cooked in which is the tagine: a clay or ceramic shallow dish with a cone-shaped lid. Did you know this style of cooking was featured in the famous *One Thousand and One Nights*, meaning this goes as far back as the ninth century? So, if you'd like to take a sensory trip to Morocco, be sure to try this aromatic stew!

 Yield: 4 servings

3 tbsp (45 ml) olive oil, divided

10½ oz (300 g) boneless chicken thighs

⅔ cup (110 g) chopped red onions

1 tbsp (9 g) minced garlic

½ tsp ground cumin

½ tsp ground coriander

½ tsp ground cinnamon

3½ oz (100 g) dried apricots

2½ cups (400 g) chickpeas, rinsed and drained

1 cup (180 g) chopped plum tomatoes

1 cup (240 ml) vegetable stock

2 tbsp (30 ml) honey

1 tsp orange zest

To Serve

1 tbsp (4 g) flat-leaf parsley, chopped

Pita bread

Mint tea

Turn on the rice cooker, set the mode to Cook and add the lid to let the rice cooker preheat for about 1 minute.

Add 2 tablespoons (30 ml) of the olive oil to the rice cooker pot and put on the lid. Let the oil heat up for 1 to 2 minutes. Add the chicken thighs to the pot and cover it again. Fry them for 3 to 4 minutes, or until they're lightly browned, before turning them over and frying them, covered, for another 3 to 4 minutes, until the other side is browned. Set them aside.

Add the remaining tablespoon (15 ml) of oil to the rice cooker pot before adding the onions. Sauté them for a minute and then add the lid. Let them fry for 3 to 4 minutes, or until the onions are softened. Then add in the garlic and sauté for another minute. Next, add in the ground cumin, coriander and cinnamon and fry for 1 to 2 minutes, or until fragrant.

At this stage, return the chicken back to the pot and throw in the apricots, chickpeas, tomatoes, stock, honey and orange zest. Give it all a good mix. Cover and cook for 20 to 25 minutes, or until the chicken is very tender. Garnish it with parsley and serve with pita and fresh mint tea, just as they do in Marrakesh!

FILIPINO PORK ADOBO

This Filipino stew is hearty and filled with chunks of melt-in-your-mouth pork belly in a beautiful medley of sweet and salty flavors. The word "adobo" was derived from the Spanish word "adobar" and means to marinate. The Philippines is composed of over 7,000 islands that are clustered into regions. Each of these regions has its own version of the adobo. You can use different meats, fish or even vegetables like eggplant to make adobo, but I prefer using pork as it tends to be the fattiest, which makes it faster to cook and makes it so tender when slow-cooked. I am making this dish with pineapple. I love this variation as the tropical fruit elevates the sweetness.

 Yield: 4 servings

For the Marinade

1 cup (240 ml) pineapple syrup

⅓ cup (80 ml) light soy sauce

¼ cup (60 ml) apple cider vinegar

1 tbsp (15 ml) oyster sauce

½ cup (80 g) diced red onions

2 tsp (10 g) whole black peppercorns

3 tbsp (25 g) minced garlic

For the Pork

2 lbs (910 g) pork belly, boneless, skin on and cut into bite-sized pieces

2 tbsp (30 ml) vegetable oil, divided

1 cup (200 g) pineapple chunks

1 cup (240 ml) water

3 bay leaves

Salt, to taste

For the marinade, in a medium-sized bowl, add the pineapple syrup, soy sauce, vinegar, oyster sauce, onions, peppercorns and garlic and stir it well. Set it aside.

To prepare the pork, rinse the pork belly pieces and dry them well. Place them in a large bowl. Pour the marinade over the pork belly and coat the pieces nicely. Cover the bowl and place it in the fridge for at least an hour. Marinate overnight if desired.

When you're ready to make the pork, turn on the rice cooker, set the mode to Cook and add the lid to let the rice cooker preheat for about 1 minute. Add 1 tablespoon (15 ml) of the vegetable oil to the rice cooker and put the lid on. Let the oil heat up over 1 to 2 minutes and then add the pineapple chunks. Caramelize them for 6 to 7 minutes with the lid closed and then set them aside.

Now add the remaining tablespoon (15 ml) of oil to the pot. Put the lid on and let it heat up for a minute. Then add the marinated pork into the pot and sauté it for about 3 to 4 minutes, or until the pork is lightly browned. Add the water and bay leaves and cook it for 30 to 45 minutes, covered, or until the pork is tender. Sprinkle the pork with a dash of salt if needed.

Then toss in the caramelized pineapple and cook everything for an additional 1 to 2 minutes before serving.

GRAINS AND SOUPS

Soups and stews are so versatile. I find nothing more comforting than a big bowl of stroganoff on a winter's night, while a light, chilled soup is equally perfect for a balmy June afternoon. Using grains like barley and beans is a great way of adding substance and texture to soups. Legumes like kidney and cannellini beans are also a fantastic way of adding plant-based protein and fiber to your diet in an affordable way.

This chapter includes creamy dishes like Hungarian Mushroom Soup (page 96) and Winter Cheese and Broccoli Soup (page 99)—which has to be my favorite way of eating broccoli—as well as spicy delights like Soulful Kimchi Jjigae (Kimchi Stew) (page 87). I am also sharing recipes for Tasty Sri Lankan Dal Parippu (Coconut Lentil Curry) (page 92) and Nourishing Chicken, Ginger and Rice Soup (page 91) which are both dishes my mum would make for me whenever I was ill as a child—they are hearty, cozy and I love them! I hope you will, too!

SPRING PEA AND GOAT CHEESE BARLEY

This dish is essentially spring on a plate. The flavor combination of peas, bacon and cheese is utterly delicious. I love using barley as it adds a nice nutty taste to your creamy risotto, and it's lower in fat and higher in fiber than Arborio rice, keeping you full for longer. Barley is also a lot harder to overcook, unlike risotto rice, which can easily turn into mush if you leave it unattended. So, barley gives you that exact al dente texture you want in a perfect plate of risotto. Fresh and frozen peas work equally well in the dish, but it is imperative that you use fresh, soft goat cheese as it can take the dish from great to outstanding!

⟵ Yield: 2–3 servings ⟶

1 tbsp (14 g) unsalted butter

2 tbsp (20 g) finely chopped white onions

1¾ oz (50 g) bacon, cut into matchsticks

1 tbsp (2 g) fresh thyme

1 cup (200 g) barley

⅓ cup (80 ml) white wine

2 cups (480 ml) chicken stock

Sea salt and freshly ground black pepper, to taste

3½ oz (100 g) frozen peas

2 oz (60 g) crumbly goat cheese, divided

1 oz (30 g) Parmesan, freshly grated

Turn on the rice cooker, set the mode to Cook and add the lid to let the rice cooker preheat for about 1 minute. Add the butter to the rice cooker, then cover it and let the butter heat up for 1 to 2 minutes. Once it melts, spread it over the base of the rice cooker.

Toss in the onions, bacon and thyme and fry them for 6 to 8 minutes with the lid on, until the onions are soft and lightly golden. Add the barley and fry it for 4 to 5 minutes, or until it's lightly browned.

Pour in the wine and stir well. Cook for 1 to 2 minutes. Then pour in the chicken stock and cook the dish for 30 to 35 minutes with the lid on, stirring midway through. Season it with salt and pepper and add in the peas. Cook for 1 to 2 minutes more.

Change the rice cooker mode to Warm and stir in 1 ounce (30 g) of goat cheese and the Parmesan. Mix it well and let it stand for at least 5 minutes. Serve the barley topped with the remaining 1 ounce (30 g) of goat cheese.

SOULFUL KIMCHI JJIGAE (KIMCHI STEW)

Kimchi jjigae, also known as kimchi stew or kimchi soup, tends to be the most common way of consuming aged kimchi. It is a staple in every Korean household and my Korean friends mentioned that they have it at home at least once a week. It is usually served in a pot at the center of the table with a range of side dishes and rice. I love kimchi jjigae as it's easy to make, yet hearty, spicy and so delicious. You can make the stew with various different meats or seafood, but my favorite is the version with pork because the fat from the meat makes the soup so much more comforting.

 Yield: 2 servings

1 tbsp (15 ml) vegetable oil

10½ oz (300 g) kimchi, cut up into bite-sized pieces

4 oz (115 g) pork belly, diced into cubes

½ cup (80 g) sliced white onions

2 tsp (4 g) gochugaru (Korean red chili pepper flakes), or to taste

1 tsp minced garlic

½ cup (120 ml) juice from kimchi

2 cups (480 ml) water

6 oz (170 g) firm tofu, sliced

2 spring onions, sliced, plus more to serve

Salt, to taste

Turn on the rice cooker, set the mode to Cook and add the lid to let the rice cooker preheat for about 1 minute. Add the vegetable oil to the rice cooker pot, cover and give the oil 1 to 2 minutes to heat up. Then add the kimchi, pork belly, onions, gochugaru and garlic to the pot and fry them for 1 to 2 minutes. Then cook, with the lid on, for 6 to 8 minutes, or until the kimchi is softened.

Now pour in the kimchi juice and add about 2 cups (480 ml) of water. Cook with the lid on for 10 to 15 minutes, or until the kimchi is very tender.

Finally, add the tofu and spring onions. Season it with salt and cook for an additional 3 to 4 minutes, or until the tofu is heated through.

Serve it hot with a garnish of chopped spring onions.

COMFORTING SAUSAGE AND BARLEY CASSEROLE

This rustic pearl barley and sausage casserole makes for a warm and hearty family dinner that's perfect for tucking into on cold, dreary nights. The flavorful sausages are slowly simmered along with the barley and vegetables in a cozy broth, and it all comes together in this wonderfully tasty, filling stew. Cumberland sausages are predominantly manufactured in England, so they might be hard to find in your country, but feel free to replace them with any other pork sausage that's peppery or spicy. You can also use cannellini or kidney beans, instead of the barley, for a lighter and more protein-rich take on this stew.

 Yield: 4 servings

2 tbsp (30 ml) olive oil, divided

1 lb (450 g) Cumberland sausages or another mild Italian pork sausage

½ cup (80 g) chopped white onions

¾ cup (100 g) diced carrots

¾ cup (75 g) sliced baby leeks

1 bay leaf

1 tbsp (2 g) fresh thyme

Salt, to taste

4 tsp (11 g) chopped garlic

1 tsp dried chili flakes

2 cups (360 g) chopped plum tomatoes

2 cups (480 ml) vegetable stock

1 cup (200 g) pearl barley

1 tsp lemon zest

2–3 sprigs fresh thyme, to serve

Turn on the rice cooker, set the mode to Cook and add the lid to let the rice cooker preheat for about 1 minute.

Add 1 tablespoon (15 ml) of the olive oil to the rice cooker pot. Put the lid on and give the oil 1 to 2 minutes to heat up. Then, add the sausages and fry them for 10 to 12 minutes, turning them every so often, until they're golden on most sides. Remove them from the pot and set them aside.

Now add the remaining 1 tablespoon (15 ml) of oil to the pot and put the lid on for 1 to 2 minutes to heat it up. Once heated, throw in the onions, carrots, leeks, bay leaf and thyme to the pan. Season them with salt and cook, covered, for 6 to 8 minutes, or until the vegetables are just beginning to soften. Stir midway through. Remove the lid, then add the garlic and chili flakes and cook for 2 to 3 minutes more.

Stir in the tomatoes, stock, pearl barley and lemon zest. Also return the sausages to the pan. Cover and cook the casserole for 30 to 35 minutes, stirring midway through, until the barley is cooked. If it seems to be getting dry, just add some water to thin it out.

Remove the bay leaf before serving the casserole with the fresh sprigs of thyme.

NOURISHING CHICKEN, GINGER AND RICE SOUP

You know how there is always that one comforting dish that you turn to whenever you're ill? For me, it's this one! The juicy chicken and tender jasmine rice make it super satisfying. The broth is cozy and anti-inflammatory. It's a soup that heals your body, mind and soul. I am using thin slices of ginger but if you'd prefer not to eat the ginger, just cut it into bigger pieces that you can pick out while you eat or before serving the soup. You can also customize this soup easily—add in spinach, finely diced carrots, sliced bok choy or any other veggies for added nutrition, texture and color.

 Yield: 2–3 servings

4 cups (960 ml) chicken stock

10 oz (300 g) boneless, skinless chicken thighs, cubed

½ oz (15 g) fresh ginger, peeled and sliced thinly

½ oz (15 g) garlic cloves, thinly sliced

¾ cup (150 g) jasmine rice, rinsed

2 tbsp (30 ml) fresh lime juice

1 tbsp (15 ml) fish sauce

Salt, to taste (optional)

2 oz (60 g) scallions, thinly sliced, to serve

3 tbsp (30 g) roasted, unsalted peanuts, to serve

½ tbsp (10 g) thinly sliced green chilies, to serve

Chili oil, to taste (optional)

Add the stock to the rice cooker, cover and set to Cook for 8 to 10 minutes, or until it comes to a boil.

When the stock comes to a boil, add the chicken, ginger, garlic and rice. Cook them for 10 to 15 minutes, or until the chicken is fully cooked. Then remove the chicken from the rice cooker pot and shred it.

Continue to cook the soup, covered, until the rice is tender. This should take another 7 to 8 minutes. Now stir in the lime juice, fish sauce and shredded chicken. Season it with salt if needed.

Serve the soup in a bowl and scatter the sliced scallions, peanuts and green chilies on top. Finish with a drizzle of chili oil, if you'd like.

TASTY SRI LANKAN DAL PARIPPU (COCONUT LENTIL CURRY)

Parippu is a staple Sri Lankan dish. This gorgeous lentil curry smells divine and offers a delicious blend of spices and creamy coconut milk. It is commonly eaten in Sri Lanka for breakfast with some warm, round rotis but works equally well as a cozy lunch or dinner dish. Parippu is usually cooked with masoor daal, or red lentils. They are incredibly rich in protein and offer many health benefits like blood sugar control, cholesterol reduction and anemia prevention. As an added bonus, red lentils also cook a whole lot faster than other types of lentils, making this my go-to meal when I'm after something tasty, warm and protein-rich that requires minimal prep.

~ Yield: 2–3 servings ~

½ cup (100 g) red lentils

1 tbsp (15 ml) coconut oil

½ tsp mustard seeds

4–5 curry leaves

½ cup (80 g) sliced red onions

4 tsp (11 g) minced garlic

½ tsp turmeric powder

1–2 green chilies, sliced

1–2 dry red chilies

¼ cup (60 ml) water, plus more as needed

½ cup (120 ml) thick coconut milk

Salt, to taste

1 tbsp (6 g) desiccated coconut, to serve

Wash the lentils thoroughly and soak them in a small bowl of water for at least 30 minutes.

Turn on the rice cooker, set the mode to Cook and add the lid to let the rice cooker preheat for about 1 minute.

Add the coconut oil to the rice cooker pot and add the lid. Let the oil heat up for 1 to 2 minutes. Once the oil has heated up, add in the mustard seeds, curry leaves, onions, garlic, turmeric, green chilies and dry red chilies. Sauté them for 30 seconds and then add the lid. Fry them, covered, for 4 to 5 minutes, or until the onions turn translucent. Remove the dry red chilies and a few of the curry leaves and set them aside; we will use these later for garnish.

Now add the drained lentils to the rice cooker pot along with the ¼ cup (60 ml) of water. Cover and cook for 15 to 20 minutes, or until the lentils are almost cooked and the water evaporates. Stir midway through and add in some more water if needed.

Now pour in the coconut milk and stir it well. Change the cooker mode to Warm and simmer for another 5 to 10 minutes, covered. Season it with salt.

Serve the dal in a bowl and top with the desiccated coconut, fried curry leaves and dry red chilies.

WARMING BACON AND POTATO SOUP

This soup, for me, is a hug in a bowl. It's rich, creamy and so comforting. Plus, it's a great way to use up potatoes; supermarkets here in England tend to sell them in big bags when I usually only need a few, so I always have a lot left over. If you want to make this soup a touch more indulgent, you can add in some shredded cheddar or Swiss cheese at the end and let it melt, incorporating it well. I've tried the cheesy version of the soup and it's honestly marvelous but I've left the cheese out in this recipe, because with the thick potatoes, the crispy bacon and the dash of cream, it feels rich and indulgent enough as is!

Yield: 6 servings

1 tbsp (14 g) unsalted butter

4 oz (115 g) bacon, diced

¼ cup (40 g) diced red onions

1 sprig fresh thyme

2 sprigs fresh rosemary

1 bay leaf

Salt and freshly ground black pepper, to taste

2 lbs (910 g) Yukon gold potatoes, peeled and cut into small pieces

2 tsp (5 g) minced garlic

3 cups (720 ml) vegetable stock, plus more if needed

½ cup (120 ml) light cream

2 tbsp (30 ml) whole grain mustard

1 tbsp (5 g) chopped scallions, to serve

Turn on the rice cooker, set the mode to Cook and add the lid to let the rice cooker preheat for about 1 minute. Add the butter to the rice cooker pot and put on the lid. Give the butter 1 to 2 minutes to melt. Toss in the diced bacon, add the lid back on and fry it for 6 to 8 minutes, or until it's crispy. Reserve 1 teaspoon of crispy bacon to use later for serving.

Now add the onions to the pot and fry them, covered, for 4 to 5 minutes, or until they soften. Then add the thyme, rosemary and bay leaf and season with salt and pepper. Cook them for a few seconds and then add the potatoes and garlic. Toss the ingredients well and pour in the stock. Cover and cook for 20 to 25 minutes, or until the potatoes are tender. At this stage, pour in the cream and add the mustard. Stir it well. Remove the bay leaf and change the rice cooker mode to Warm.

Use a hand blender to carefully blend about half of the soup. We essentially want a mix of very silky and slightly chunky textures in the soup. Alternatively, you can just remove half of the soup with a ladle and add it to a blender. Blend it until it's smooth and return it to the pot. Mix it well.

Add more salt and pepper if needed. Serve the soup in bowls topped with the reserved crispy bacon and scallions.

HUNGARIAN MUSHROOM SOUP

I love Budapest; it's one of my favorite cities in Eastern Europe. The healing thermal waters, the resplendent architecture and the cozy little cafés make for a memorable vacation. A dish that I clearly remember having in an elegant restaurant by the mighty river Danube is this mushroom soup. It's soul-warming, soothing and laced with paprika. I love the earthiness of the mushrooms and the caramelized onions, and I knew I had to make it myself. It's now a soup I cook every month because that's just how much I love it and I hope you do, too. Just make sure to use good-quality, meaty mushrooms as they are the hero of the dish. Shiitake or cremini are ideal, but white button mushrooms also work well.

Yield: 4 servings

¼ cup (56 g) unsalted butter, divided

1 lb (450 g) mushrooms, sliced, divided (you can use white, shiitake or a mix of wild mushrooms)

⅓ cup (55 g) diced white onions

1 tbsp (7 g) paprika

3 cups (720 ml) vegetable stock

3 tbsp (45 ml) soy sauce

3 tbsp (25 g) flour

1 cup (240 ml) whole milk

½ cup (120 ml) sour cream, plus more to serve

1 tbsp (15 ml) lemon juice

1 tbsp (3 g) chopped fresh dill

¼ cup (15 g) chopped fresh parsley, plus more to serve

Salt and freshly ground black pepper, to taste

Turn on the rice cooker, set the mode to Cook and add the lid to let the rice cooker preheat for about 1 minute.

Add in 2 teaspoons (10 g) of butter, cover and let the butter melt for 1 to 2 minutes. Once it has melted, add in about 2 ounces (50 g) of mushroom slices and sauté them for 1 to 2 minutes, before putting on the lid and frying them for 8 to 10 minutes more, until they are golden brown and slightly crisp. Stir them midway through. Then set them aside. We will use these when serving the soup.

Now add the remaining 9 teaspoons (45 g) of butter to the pot. Add the lid and let the butter melt, which should take 1 to 2 minutes. Toss in the onions, sauté them for a minute and then cover the pot. Fry them for 5 to 6 minutes, or until they have softened. Then add the remaining 14 ounces (400 g) of mushrooms and the paprika. Fry them, covered, for 10 to 15 minutes, or until the liquid from the mushrooms has been released and evaporated. Make sure to stir them every few minutes.

Pour in the stock and soy sauce. Cover and cook for 5 to 6 minutes, or until the soup begins to reduce. Meanwhile, in a small bowl, mix the flour with the whole milk. Then add it to the rice cooker pot. Cover it and continue to cook for another 8 to 10 minutes, or until the soup thickens.

Turn off the rice cooker and mix in the sour cream, lemon juice, dill and parsley. Season it with salt and pepper. Serve with some more parsley, the fried mushroom slices and a dollop of sour cream.

WINTER CHEESE AND BROCCOLI SOUP

Whoever invented this dish is a genius, as this has to be the tastiest way of eating broccoli. There's something so uniquely cozy about this soup. It uses minimal ingredients but gives you maximum flavor. It is rich and luscious but without all the guilt as it's loaded with vitamin- and iron-packed broccoli. This soup really is filled with all the good stuff. There are a few different variations of broccoli soup but I like to make it without a roux, as the roux can sometimes make the soup grainy or curdled. This version is one I have tried and tested and is sure to give you an extra creamy and smooth texture. And for any keto readers out there (or if you're having keto guests over), this is the perfect dish for you!

 Yield: 2–3 servings

3 cups (720 ml) vegetable stock

4 cups (350 g) fresh broccoli, cut up into florets

4 tbsp (56 g) unsalted butter, divided

¼ cup (40 g) diced white onions

¾ cup (100 g) diced carrots

1 tbsp (9 g) minced garlic

½ tsp cayenne pepper

1 cup (240 ml) heavy cream

1 oz (30 g) cream cheese

1 tsp Dijon mustard

3 cups (300 g) sharp cheddar cheese, shredded, plus more to serve

4 slices (100 g) Swiss cheese, shredded

¼ tsp nutmeg

1 tsp parsley

Sea salt and freshly ground black pepper, to taste

Add the stock to the rice cooker. Cover and cook it for 8 to 10 minutes, or until it comes to a boil. Add the broccoli and cook it for 6 to 8 minutes, or until the broccoli is tender. Take the broccoli out and set it aside. Reserve about 2 cups (480 ml) of the stock. We will use it later in the soup.

Clean and dry the rice cooker completely. Turn on the rice cooker, set the mode to Cook and add the lid to let the rice cooker preheat for about 1 minute.

Add in the butter. Put the lid on and give the butter a minute or two to melt. Once it melts, toss in the diced onions and carrots and sauté them for 1 to 2 minutes. Then add the lid and fry them for 4 to 5 minutes more, stirring occasionally, until the onions have softened. Now add the garlic and cayenne pepper and fry them for 1 to 2 minutes, or until they're fragrant.

Pour in 1 cup (240 ml) of the reserved stock, the heavy cream, cream cheese and mustard and stir well. Cover and cook for 5 to 6 minutes, or until it reaches a simmer. Now slowly add in the shredded cheddar and Swiss cheeses, stirring gently until they are fully incorporated. Now add in the cooked broccoli and the remaining 1 cup (240 ml) of stock that you had previously set aside. Sprinkle in the nutmeg and parsley. Season the soup with salt and pepper and mix well. Change the rice cooker to the Warm mode. You can now use a hand blender to blend all or some of the soup, to your preference.

Serve it with some more shredded cheddar cheese.

LOADED TACO SOUP

Everyone loves tacos! Taco nights are always a hit. But tacos aren't the quickest to make—you need to get the meat sizzling in a pan, warm up the tortillas in another and prep your guacamole on the side. But this soup brings you the flavors of tacos, without all the fuss. This taco soup is zesty, packed with protein and totally crave-worthy. It reminds me somewhat of a chili con carne but with a lot more excitement and color with the toppings: avocado slices, crispy tortilla chips and sour cream. I cannot think of another soup that offers such a wonderful mix of textures. It truly is a savior on cold, dreary nights.

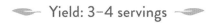 Yield: 3–4 servings

For the Taco Seasoning

2 tbsp (12 g) chili powder

2 tsp (3 g) ground cumin

1 tsp salt, or to taste

1 tsp freshly ground black pepper, or to taste

1 tsp cornstarch

1 tsp smoked paprika (or substitute hot or sweet paprika)

½ tsp garlic powder

½ tsp onion powder

½ tsp crushed red pepper flakes, or to taste

For the Soup

1 tbsp (15 ml) olive oil

12 oz (340 g) canned diced tomatoes

For the taco seasoning, in a small bowl, mix the chili powder, cumin, salt, pepper, cornstarch, paprika, garlic powder, onion powder and red pepper flakes together and set it aside.

To begin the soup, turn on the rice cooker, set the mode to Cook and add the lid to let the rice cooker preheat for about 1 minute. Pour in the olive oil and put the lid on. Let the oil heat up for 1 to 2 minutes and then throw in the diced tomatoes and cook them for 3 to 4 minutes with the lid back on.

(continued)

8 oz (225 g) canned black beans, drained and rinsed

8 oz (225 g) canned pinto beans, drained and rinsed

1 cup (240 ml) vegetable broth

½ cup (120 ml) water

½ cup (80 g) canned sweet corn, drained

2 tbsp (15 g) Taco Seasoning, previously made

For the Garnish

⅓ cup (50 g) diced avocado

½ cup (40 g) crumbled feta cheese

4–5 tortilla chips

½ tbsp (4 g) grated cheddar cheese

2 tsp (5 g) finely diced red onions

1 tbsp (8 g) sliced jalapeños

1–2 lime wedges

1 tbsp (15 ml) sour cream

Add the black beans and pinto beans to the pot. Pour in the vegetable broth and water. Stir them well. Then add the corn and taco seasoning. Cover and cook the soup for 15 to 20 minutes, or until fully heated through.

Pour the soup into bowls and top with the avocado, crumbled feta cheese, tortilla chips, shredded cheddar cheese, red onions, jalapeños, lime wedges and sour cream. You don't have to add them all—feel free to pick and choose the ones you like most!

CREAMY CANNELLINI AND WILD RICE SOUP

This is a wonderfully creamy, full-bodied white bean soup that is guaranteed to warm your soul on a cold, rainy day. It is cozy and so rustic. I like adding wild rice to it as it lends a nutty, earthy taste as well as a lot more texture to the soup. Not to mention, wild rice is lower in calories and higher in fiber, antioxidants and protein in comparison to all other types of rice, helping make the soup nourishing and filling. The miso paste adds a touch of umami to the soup which works well with the slightly buttery, nutty tones in the dish. The blended cashews make this soup extra comforting and luscious.

— Yield: 2 servings —

For the Cannellini Cashew Cream

½ cup (70 g) raw cashews, soaked overnight, then drained

¼ cup (45 g) cooked cannellini beans, drained and rinsed

1 cup (240 ml) almond milk

1 tbsp (8 g) miso paste

1 tsp Dijon mustard

For the Soup

1 tbsp (15 ml) olive oil

½ cup (80 g) chopped white onions

½ cup (50 g) chopped celery

½ cup (65 g) chopped carrots

4 oz (115 g) mushrooms, sliced

Salt and freshly ground black pepper, to taste

For the cannellini cashew cream, in a blender, add the drained cashews, cannellini beans, almond milk, miso paste and Dijon mustard. Blend until it's smooth. Set it aside.

For the soup, turn on the rice cooker, set the mode to Cook and add the lid to let the rice cooker preheat for about 1 minute. Add the olive oil to the rice cooker pot. Put the lid on. Give the oil 1 to 2 minutes to heat up, then add the onions, celery, carrots and mushrooms and season them with salt and pepper. Add the lid and fry the vegetables for 8 to 10 minutes, or until the mushrooms are tender.

(continued)

CREAMY CANNELLINI AND WILD RICE SOUP (CONT.)

1 tbsp (9 g) minced garlic

1 tbsp (4 g) dried thyme

1 bay leaf

1 tbsp (3 g) fresh rosemary

½ cup (90 g) cooked cannellini beans, drained and rinsed

½ cup (100 g) wild rice

2 cups (480 ml) vegetable broth

2 tsp (10 ml) fresh lemon juice

1 tbsp (3 g) fresh parsley, to serve

Now add the garlic, thyme, bay leaf, rosemary, cannellini beans, wild rice and broth. Cover it and cook for 20 to 25 minutes, or until the wild rice is fully cooked.

Stir the cannellini cashew cream into the soup as well as the fresh lemon juice. Remove the bay leaf before serving the soup with chopped parsley.

FISH AND SEAFOOD

I love fish—it's lean, rich in protein and packed with omega-3 fatty acids. But even more importantly, it is versatile. I feel that there are fish and seafood dishes to suit every occasion—go for a rich fish curry on a cold winter night or some steamed salmon if you're after a light lunch.

Fresh fish is as fragile in its flavor as in its texture. It is easy to overcook fish and seafood—you can go from underdone to overcooked and dry within seconds. So, it is an ideal candidate for the rice cooker, that you can use to gently poach the fish or to steam it on a timer to get beautiful, flaky fish each time.

In this chapter, I'll be sharing some fantastic fish dishes that transport me to the sea. Get a taste of New Orleans with the Cajun Lobster Boil (page 111) or be transported to the coasts of India with my coconut-y Tangy Goan Fish Curry (page 108)! No matter which dish you choose to whip up, you'll be in for a flavorful seaside journey!

TANGY GOAN FISH CURRY

Goa, on India's beautiful west coast, is the ultimate tourist destination with sun, sea, sand and good food! Goan fish curries are generally made with three key components: coconut, spices and something to give the curry a distinct slight sourness, usually from tamarind, but vinegar, kokum or other citrusy ingredients can also be used. This hot and sour combination is unique to Goan curries and is expected to have been derived from the Portuguese, who ruled in Goa for over 450 years. The rice cooker is ideal for making fish curries like this—no need to fry or bake the fish separately, just simmer it to perfection in the curry base. It's a one-pot, foolproof and fantastic way to prep fish.

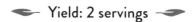 Yield: 2 servings

For the Masala

3 tbsp (21 g) Kashmiri chili powder

2 tbsp (17 g) minced garlic

1 tsp whole peppercorns

1 tbsp (6 g) whole coriander seeds

1 tsp cumin seeds

1 tbsp (16 g) tamarind paste

1 tsp turmeric powder

½ cup (48 g) grated fresh coconut

1 cup (240 ml) coconut milk

For the Curry

2 tbsp (30 g) coconut oil

1½ tbsp (11 g) finely minced fresh ginger

½ cup (80 g) finely chopped red onions

½ cup (90 g) finely chopped plum tomatoes

Salt, to taste

9 oz (255 g) tilapia fillets

1 cup (240 ml) water

8–10 curry leaves

For the masala, in a blender, add the Kashmiri chili powder, garlic, peppercorns, coriander seeds, cumin seeds, tamarind paste, turmeric powder, grated coconut and coconut milk and blend until you get a smooth paste. Set it aside.

To begin the curry, turn on the rice cooker, set the mode to Cook and add the lid to let the rice cooker preheat for about 1 minute. Add the coconut oil to the pan. Put the lid on and let the oil heat up, which should take 1 to 2 minutes, and then add the ginger and onions to the pot. Sauté them for a minute and then put the lid back on. Cook them for 3 to 4 minutes, or until they are a light golden brown.

Now add the tomatoes. Fry them for 30 seconds and then cook them, covered, for 6 to 8 minutes, until they break down easily with the back of a spoon. Stir them midway through. Add the masala at this stage and season it with salt. Fry the masala for a minute and then close the lid. Let it cook for 8 to 10 minutes, or until it comes to a boil.

When boiling, open the lid to add the tilapia and 1 cup (240 ml) of water. Give it a good mix. Cook, covered, for 10 to 12 minutes more, or until the fish is flaky. Then sprinkle in the curry leaves and close the lid. Set the rice cooker mode to Warm and let the curry sit in the cooker for 4 to 5 minutes to help infuse the flavors better before serving.

CAJUN LOBSTER BOIL

What is the one thing more decadent than lobster? Lobster doused in a load of hot melted butter! It really doesn't get any more impressive than this for your dinner party guests. Yes, I admit—this does get a bit messy to eat, but it's a worthwhile, delicious, fabulous kind of messy. I am using a whole lobster, but feel free to use lobster tails or a selection of other seafood like prawns, crab claws and crayfish. I find the garlic and spicy Cajun seasoning to be perfect with the sweet, soft lobster meat. It gives the right level of kick without taking away from the buttery deliciousness of the lobster.

 Yield: 2 servings

1½ lbs (680 g) lobster

7 oz (200 g) corn on the cob, cut into ¾-inch (2-cm) pieces

1 lemon, halved

For the Cajun Seasoning

½ tbsp (4 g) sea salt

½ tbsp (3 g) sweet paprika

½ tbsp (3 g) garlic powder

1 tsp ground white pepper

1 tsp onion powder

½ tsp ground cumin

½ tsp cayenne pepper

½ tsp dried oregano

½ tsp dried thyme

For the Boil

5 tbsp (70 g) unsalted butter, melted

3 tbsp (25 g) minced garlic

2 tbsp (30 ml) hot sauce

To prepare the lobster, fill the rice cooker with 3 cups (720 ml) of water and set the mode to Cook. When the water is boiling, lift up the rice cooker lid and add the lobster, corn and lemon halves. Cover and cook for 8 to 10 minutes. Once fully cooked, the shell of the lobster will turn a vivid red. Drain the lobster and corn and set them aside.

To make the Cajun seasoning, in a small bowl, mix the salt, paprika, garlic powder, white pepper, onion powder, cumin, cayenne pepper, oregano and thyme. Set it aside.

Empty the rice cooker pot and dry it fully. Turn on the rice cooker, set the mode to Cook and add the lid to let the rice cooker preheat for about 1 minute.

Add the butter and put the lid on. Let the butter melt for 1 to 2 minutes, then add the garlic and sauté it for 1 to 2 minutes, or until it starts to turn golden. Throw in the Cajun seasoning and the hot sauce. Mix it well and then add in the lobster and corn. Toss them together and serve the dish hot.

MILK-POACHED COD WITH LEEKS

Poaching is a technique I seriously swear by for cooking fish. Perfectly poached fish is extremely tender and just melts in your mouth. It is a fuss-free technique that helps lock the moisture in the fish and elevates it. I prefer using whole milk instead of water or stock as the poaching liquid because the higher fat content of the milk makes it better at absorbing the flavors from the herbs being used in the dish. You could also try adding some light cream or half-and-half to give you a richer poaching liquid. Here I am using cod, a mild white flaky fish that is high in protein and several B-vitamins, but low in calories and carbs.

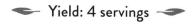 Yield: 4 servings

1 lb (450 g) baby potatoes

5–6 large cloves garlic, peeled and divided

3 cups (720 ml) whole milk

9 oz (255 g) leeks, white and pale green parts only, halved lengthwise

1 bay leaf

Salt, to taste

1¼ lbs (565 g) skinless cod fillets (aim for 4 fillets of 6-oz [170-g] each)

2 tbsp (30 g) mascarpone cheese

1 tbsp (15 ml) olive oil, for drizzling

Freshly ground pink peppercorns, to serve

4–5 sprigs fresh dill, to serve

Add the potatoes and 4 cups (960 ml) of water to the rice cooker along with 2 cloves of garlic, smashed. Turn on the rice cooker and set it to Cook. Cover and let the potatoes cook for 25 to 30 minutes, until they can be easily pierced with a fork. Remove the garlic cloves and drain the potatoes. Set them aside.

Now dry out the rice cooker pot completely and pour in the milk. Add the lid and turn the device to Cook. Let it heat up for 1 to 2 minutes and then add in the leeks, bay leaf and remaining 3 to 4 cloves of garlic. Season them generously with salt and cook for 6 to 8 minutes, or until the leeks begin to soften.

Gently slide the cod into the infused milk with the leeks and poach, with the lid on, until the flesh is cooked through and is beginning to flake, which should take 8 to 10 minutes. Then carefully transfer the fish fillets to your serving plates. Add the potatoes on the side.

Add the mascarpone cheese to the poaching liquid and stir it in. Season it with salt. Spoon this sauce over the fish and the potatoes on your serving plates. Drizzle the fish with some olive oil, salt, pink pepper and dill.

STEAMED COD IN MUSTARD SAUCE

Being of Bengali heritage, I couldn't not share the dish that is perhaps the most popular and emblematic of Bengali cuisine: Shorshe Ilish. "Shorshe" refers to mustard paste while "Ilish," also known as "Hilsa," is a type of Indian herring with a distinct, delicious taste. But because Hilsa is difficult to get outside the Indian subcontinent, I decided to make this dish using cod. The tangy mustard paste is balanced beautifully by the slightly sweet, flaky cod. If you'd like a milder version, simply cut down on the amount of green chilies and add some desiccated coconut to the mustard paste, instead. For me, this dish is an homage to my childhood and never fails to indulge me. Here's hoping you'll enjoy it, too!

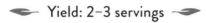 Yield: 2–3 servings

For the Mustard Paste

2 tbsp (12 g) whole yellow mustard seeds, soaked in ¼ cup (60 ml) water for an hour

1 green chili, sliced

½ tsp salt, or to taste

½ tsp granulated sugar

For the Fish

1 lb (450 g) cod fillets

1 tsp salt, plus more to taste

1 tsp turmeric

2 tbsp (30 ml) mustard oil

1–2 sliced green chilies, or to taste

White rice, cooked, to serve

For the mustard paste, in a blender, add the mustard seeds along with the water they were soaked in. Also add the chili, salt and sugar. Blend them until smooth and set the paste aside.

To begin making the fish, in a medium-sized bowl, marinate the cod fillets with 1 teaspoon of salt and the turmeric and set them aside for at least 30 minutes.

After marinating, place the fish fillets in a shallow bowl that can fit in your steamer basket. Pour the mustard paste and mustard oil over the fillets. Coat them well and top them with the green chilies.

Add 2 cups (480 ml) of water to the rice cooker. Cover and set the rice cooker to Cook for 8 to 10 minutes, or until the water comes to a boil. Lift the lid and place the bowl with the fish in the steamer basket and position it above the water in the cooker. Cover and cook the fish for 10 to 12 minutes.

We will finish cooking on low heat. Turn the rice cooker to the Warm mode and let the fish steam on low for another 8 to 10 minutes. Serve the dish with plain white rice.

GARLICKY PRAWNS PIL PIL

Spanish Prawns Pil Pil is a popular Andalucian tapas dish. It is normally made to order in restaurants and served with some crusty bread to mop up all that good sauce. This tapas dish is ridiculously easy to prepare and requires very few ingredients. So, it is important to use high-quality ingredients and let the produce shine through. You don't want to use cooked prawns for this. You could use frozen prawns, but I am using fresh king prawns from my local fishmongers. Also, good-quality extra virgin olive oil, ideally Spanish, is essential for this dish.

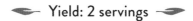 Yield: 2 servings

1 cup (240 ml) extra virgin olive oil

¼ cup (34 g) finely sliced garlic

2 tsp (4 g) dried chili flakes

2 tsp (4 g) smoked sweet paprika

10½ oz (300 g) king prawns, peeled and cleaned

1 tbsp (4 g) finely chopped flat-leaf parsley, to serve

Salt, to taste

Sliced bread, to serve

Turn on the rice cooker, set the mode to Cook and add the lid to let the rice cooker preheat for about 1 minute.

Add the olive oil to the rice cooker pot. Put on the lid. Give the oil 1 to 2 minutes to heat up. Once heated, add the sliced garlic. Sauté the garlic for 30 seconds and then put the lid on. Fry it for 1 to 2 minutes, or until the garlic starts to change color, then add the chili flakes and paprika. Fry it for 30 seconds more, stirring well.

Next, add the prawns and fry them for 1 to 2 minutes on each side, until they're fully cooked and opaque.

Sprinkle the prawns with the parsley, season them with salt, then serve them hot with a side of sliced bread for dipping.

SMALL PLATES

This chapter of the book is an amalgamation of dishes that are perfect as starters, snacks and sides. You've got dishes like the Soft Khaman Dhokla (page 127) and Spanish Chorizo in Red Wine (page 134), which are perfect for sharing with friends over a round of drinks. Then there are recipes like Korean Corn Cheese (page 133), Sichuan Chili Garlic Eggplant (page 120) and Juicy Mushroom and Wild Garlic Dumplings (page 124), which are all fabulous side dishes that make everyday vegetables the hero and are the perfect way to incorporate more vegetables into your diet.

I also used this chapter to share a little love for tofu and paneer. I remember thinking that these foods were super plain and lacking in flavor. However, over the years, I've grown to love them. They're extremely versatile, protein-rich and so delicious. They readily absorb spices and seasonings and work beautifully in a range of recipes from stir-fries to blended dips. I have included some of my favorite dishes in this chapter including Sichuan-style Fragrant Mapo Tofu (page 127) and Nutritious Palak Paneer (page 123) that are absolutely addictive and among my favorite vegetarian curries.

The versatility of the humble rice cooker comes through quite clearly in this chapter. You use it to steam eggplant and dumplings, to make curries and to slowly simmer chorizo. Also, I often prepare a lot of these dishes as starters and sides and like to work on them while cooking my mains. So, it is very handy to use the rice cooker as it requires a lot less monitoring. I just leave the dishes to cook and they're all ready to be served when the timer goes off.

SICHUAN CHILI GARLIC EGGPLANT

Eggplant is such a versatile vegetable to cook with. I love it fried, grilled and baked, but one of my favorite ways to eat it is steamed! Steamed eggplant is known for its silky texture and its ability to soak up flavors.

My recipe is inspired by the Sichuan recipe Yu Xiang, which translates to "fish-fragrant eggplant." Most Sichuan dishes involve wok frying at high temperatures, but I have adapted the recipe to a rice cooker—this allows me to tap into the delicious flavor profile while steaming the eggplants instead. It involves soft, silky slices of eggplant smothered in super-addictive spicy chili garlic sauce. It is easy to make and feels substantial, so it is equally wonderful as both a weeknight dinner and as a side for a big weekend feast.

 Yield: 2 servings

10½ oz (300 g) eggplant, cut into wedges

2 tbsp (30 ml) vegetable oil

¼ tsp sesame oil, plus more to serve

1 tsp ground Sichuan peppercorns

1 tsp grated fresh ginger

½ tsp sesame seeds, plus more to serve

2 tbsp (30 ml) chili oil, plus more to serve

1 tbsp (15 ml) tahini or peanut butter

1½ tbsp (21 ml) soy sauce, or to taste

1 tbsp (15 ml) rice wine vinegar

2 tsp (10 g) granulated sugar

1 tbsp (7 g) finely chopped long hot green peppers

5 tsp (15 g) minced garlic

¼ cup (12 g) finely chopped scallions, divided

1 tbsp (15 g) chili bean paste

½ cup (120 ml) vegetable stock

1 tbsp (10 g) peanuts, crushed, to serve

½ tsp sesame seeds, to serve

Slice the eggplant wedges into thin slices. Arrange them on a heatproof plate. Add 2 cups (480 ml) of water to the rice cooker pot. Cover and set it to Cook for 8 to 10 minutes, or until the water comes to a boil. Open the lid and place the plate with the eggplant in the steamer basket. Cover it and cook for 10 to 12 minutes, or until the eggplant is soft. Then remove the eggplant.

Dry the rice cooker pot completely. Turn on the rice cooker, set the mode to Cook and add the lid to let the rice cooker preheat for about 1 minute. Add the vegetable oil and sesame oil to the pot. Cover and let the oils heat up for 1 to 2 minutes. Once the oils heat up, add in the Sichuan peppercorns, ginger and sesame seeds. Stir them for 30 seconds, or until the ginger is fragrant, and then stir in the chili oil, tahini, soy sauce, vinegar and sugar.

Cook the sauce for 1 to 2 minutes and then stir in the green peppers, garlic, 2 tablespoons (6 g) of the scallions and the chili bean paste. Add the stock, put on the lid and cook the sauce for 2 to 3 minutes, or until it thickens slightly.

Toss the steamed eggplant in the sauce and then plate the meal. Drizzle some more chili oil over the dish if you'd like and serve it with the remaining 2 tablespoons (6 g) scallions, peanuts and sesame seeds.

NUTRITIOUS PALAK PANEER (COTTAGE CHEESE AND SPINACH CURRY)

Who knew a dish packed with spinach could be this rich and creamy! This is hands down my favorite way to eat spinach: in a buttery, smooth gravy studded with soft, fresh paneer. What's even better is that the recipe uses blanched and blended spinach, so its color and nutrients remain mostly preserved. The dash of cream balances out the slight bitterness of the spinach and makes it even more silky and luxurious. It's easy, nutritious and truly a delight for the senses.

 Yield: 4 servings

1 lb (450 g) fresh spinach

2–3 green chilies, sliced

3 tbsp (45 ml) vegetable oil

½ tsp cumin seeds

⅓ cup (55 g) chopped red onions

1 tbsp (7 g) grated fresh ginger

¼ cup (34 g) minced garlic

½ cup (120 ml) water

Salt, to taste

¼ tsp garam masala

7 oz (200 g) paneer, cubed

4 tbsp (60 ml) heavy cream

1 tsp kasoori methi (dried fenugreek leaves), to serve (optional; see Note)

Remove the stems from the spinach and wash thoroughly in running water. Prepare a small bowl of salted boiling water and a small bowl of cold water. Blanch the spinach in boiling water for 2 to 3 minutes. Then add it to the bowl of chilled water for about 30 seconds. Squeeze out the excess water.

In a blender, add the blanched spinach along with the green chilies and blend them into a fine paste. Set it aside.

Turn on the rice cooker, set the mode to Cook and add the lid to let the rice cooker preheat for about 1 minute. Add the vegetable oil to the rice cooker and put the lid on. Once the oil heats up, add the cumin seeds. Fry them, with the lid back on, for 20 to 30 seconds, or until they become fragrant. Then add the onions, ginger and garlic and sauté them for a minute. Then fry them, covered, for 5 to 6 minutes, or until they're golden.

Pour the spinach puree, along with ½ cup (120 ml) of water, into the pot and stir well. Cover and cook for 3 to 4 minutes, or until the spinach begins to bubble. Season it with salt and add the garam masala. Give it a stir before adding the paneer cubes. Cover and cook the dish for 30 seconds to a minute. You want to just heat the paneer but not overcook it, as that could make it chewy.

Change the rice cooker mode to Warm and then stir in the cream. Optionally, sprinkle some crushed kasoori methi over your palak paneer to serve it.

NOTE: *Kasoori methi, or dried fenugreek leaves, have a distinctive nutty, savory and slightly bitter taste. You can find them in Indian supermarkets and spice shops.*

JUICY MUSHROOM AND WILD GARLIC DUMPLINGS

Whenever spring hits, I get excited for wild garlic season because as a garlic lover, I can't think of a tastier herb.

I love dumplings with a juicy, garlicky filling. With that in mind, I experimented with reducing the amount of minced garlic, replacing it with some fresh wild garlic, and I am very happy to report that it works a treat! I also wanted to keep the dumplings vegetarian so we can highlight our aromatic spring herb in this recipe. If you are struggling to find wild garlic, these dumplings work well with spinach and some more minced garlic. I also made my dumpling wrappers from scratch, as they are a lot more pliable and easier to wrap, but if you're pressed for time, premade dumpling wrappers can also do the job.

 Yield: 3–4 servings

For the Filling

1 tbsp (15 ml) vegetable oil

2 tbsp (17 g) washed and finely chopped wild garlic

2 tbsp (17 g) minced ginger

1 tbsp (9 g) minced garlic

¼ cup (40 g) finely chopped red onions

1 cup (70 g) finely diced shiitake or button mushrooms

½ cup (35 g) finely chopped cabbage

½ cup (65 g) finely chopped carrots

1 tsp ground white pepper

2 tbsp (30 ml) soy sauce

3 tbsp (45 ml) Shaoxing wine or dry sherry

1 tsp granulated sugar

Salt, to taste

2 tbsp (18 g) sesame oil

For the filling, turn on the rice cooker, set the mode to Cook and add the lid to let the rice cooker preheat for about 1 minute. Add in the vegetable oil. Put on the lid and give the oil 1 to 2 minutes to heat up.

Next, add in the wild garlic, ginger, minced garlic, onions, mushrooms, cabbage and carrots. Stir them for a few seconds and season them with the white pepper, soy sauce, Shaoxing wine, sugar and salt. Fry them for 8 to 10 minutes, or until the mixture is soft. Then drizzle with the sesame oil and mix well. Remove the mixture from the rice cooker and set it aside.

(continued)

JUICY MUSHROOM AND
WILD GARLIC DUMPLINGS (CONT.)

For the Dumpling Wrappers

½ cup (120 ml) water

2 cups (250 g) all-purpose flour, plus more for dusting

For the Garnish

2 tbsp (30 ml) chili oil

1 tbsp (3 g) finely chopped spring onions

> **NOTES:** *If you struggle with pleating your dumplings, you can fold the wrapper in half to make a half-moon shape. To help seal the dumplings, the wrapper edge should be lightly brushed with water.*
>
> *Alternatively, you can also use a dumpling mold—they are an affordable, simple kitchen tool which can be used to create more elaborate dumpling pleats.*

For the dumpling wrappers, in a medium-sized mixing bowl, add the water to the flour gradually. I use a combination of boiling water and regular water in a 2:1 ratio for a less resilient texture, which is better suited to steamed dumplings. Also, you might need to use 1 to 2 teaspoons (5 to 10 ml) more or less of the water depending on the type of flour you're using and how humid your kitchen is. With this in mind, I suggest adding the water bit by bit instead of all in one go.

Gently mix the water and flour together with a pair of chopsticks or a spatula until there is no more loose flour. Then tip the dough onto a clean surface and knead it with your hands. Leave it to rest in a bowl, covered with a damp cloth, for 10 to 15 minutes, then knead it again into a smooth dough. Cover and rest the dough for an additional 30 to 60 minutes, until it becomes soft.

Divide the dough into 25 to 30 separate, equal-sized portions. Roll them out into discs, using a dusting of flour. You can roll out all the wrappers in one go and then stack them with a sprinkle of flour between the wrappers to prevent them from sticking and freeze them if you would like to have them for future use. Or, you can just roll a wrapper at a time, stuff it and pleat it before moving on to rolling out the next wrapper. In this case, keep the rest of the dough in a bowl covered with a damp cloth, so it doesn't dry out.

Add about 1 tablespoon (10 g) of stuffing in the middle of each wrapper and then pleat (see Notes). Place the pleated dumplings on a plate dusted with flour and keep them covered with a damp cloth to avoid them drying out.

Add 2 cups (480 ml) of water to the rice cooker. Put the lid on, set it to Cook and give it 8 to 10 minutes to let it come to a boil. Place the dumplings in the steamer basket. Cover and cook them for 12 to 15 minutes, or until the dumplings are done. To check if they are done, prick one of the dumplings with a toothpick and see if it comes out clean. If not, let them stand in the steamer basket for a few more minutes. Serve the dumplings with the chili oil and spring onions.

SOFT KHAMAN DHOKLA
(SAVORY GRAM FLOUR CAKE)

Dhokla is a popular snack from the state of Gujarat on the western coast of India. It is soft, fluffy and makes for the ideal snack any time of day. Think of it as a super light, savory version of a sponge cake. Now traditionally, you'd ferment the gram (chickpea) flour and yogurt batter for several hours, in preparation of this dish. It is that fermentation indeed, which gives it the complexity of flavor and that airy, spongy texture. But you can simulate a similar effect to that fermentation process by using baking soda.

 Yield: 3–4 servings

For the Dhokla

1 cup (120 g) chickpea flour

2 tbsp (20 g) semolina

Pinch of asafoetida (hing) (optional; see Note)

1 tsp lemon juice

½ tsp turmeric

⅓ tsp salt

1 tbsp (15 g) granulated sugar

1 tsp grated fresh ginger

1 tsp chopped green chilies

4 tbsp (60 ml) vegetable oil, divided

¾ cup (180 ml) water

1 tsp baking soda

To begin making the dhokla batter, sift the chickpea flour into a large bowl. Add the semolina, asafoetida (if using), lemon juice, turmeric, salt, sugar, ginger, chilies, 3 tablespoons (45 ml) of the vegetable oil and ¾ cup (180 ml) of water. Mix the ingredients well until no lumps remain. You might need to add more or less water—add it a teaspoon or so at a time until you reach a pouring consistency. Set the batter aside and keep the bowl covered.

We will now steam our dhokla. For this, pour 4 cups (960 ml) of water into the rice cooker pot. Set the rice cooker to Cook and cover. Let the water come to a boil, which should take about 10 to 12 minutes. At this stage, grease a metal or plastic tray or container with the remaining 1 tablespoon (15 ml) of oil.

Add the baking soda to the chickpea flour batter and stir well to begin fermentation. Pour the batter into the greased container and add a lid. Place the container in the steaming basket of the rice cooker. Put on the rice cooker lid and steam the mixture for 15 to 20 minutes. Check if it's done by seeing if a knife comes out clean from the batter. If not, steam it for 4 to 5 minutes more.

Once it's done, set the container with the dhokla aside. Dry out the rice cooker pot completely.

(continued)

SOFT KHAMAN DHOKLA
(SAVORY GRAM FLOUR CAKE) (CONT.)

For the Tempering

1 tbsp (15 ml) vegetable oil

1 tsp mustard seeds

10–12 curry leaves

2 tsp (3 g) chopped green chilies

2 tbsp (30 g) granulated sugar

½ cup (120 ml) water

To prepare the tempering, turn on the rice cooker, set the mode to Cook and add the lid to let the rice cooker preheat for about 1 minute. Add the vegetable oil to the rice cooker pot. Put on the lid and heat the oil for 2 to 3 minutes, until it is shimmering hot. Add the mustard seeds and curry leaves. Fry them for 2 to 3 minutes, with the lid on, or until the seeds start crackling. Then add the chilies, put the lid back on and fry them for another minute. Add the sugar and let it dissolve. Then add in ½ cup (120 ml) of water.

Remove the dhokla from the container by flipping it onto a greased tray and then cut it into squares of 2 x 2 inches (5 x 5 cm). Pour the tempering water over the dhokla and dig in.

NOTE: *I have kept the asafoetida optional as it does have an intense aroma, but a pinch of it can help balance out the flavors in a dish. Asafoetida, or hing, comes from the resin of giant fennel plants and adds a hint of umami to the dish. You can find this spice in Indian supermarkets or online.*

FRAGRANT MAPO TOFU (SILKEN TOFU WITH FERMENTED BEAN CURD AND CHILIES)

Mapo tofu is one of the most popular dishes from the Sichuan province. Creamy, silken tofu cubes sit in an aromatic, fiery and lip-smackingly delicious sauce. Although the dish is traditionally made with ground pork, I wanted to share a vegan version which I think is equally wonderful! You can adjust the recipe as you like but the two absolutely essential ingredients needed for this dish are Sichuan peppercorns and spicy bean sauce, which give it that numbing taste and spicy, fermented flavor. If there's one dish I'd make to convert any tofu skeptics out there, it would be this one!

 Yield: 2 servings

¼ cup (60 ml) vegetable oil

1 tbsp (7 g) Sichuan peppercorns

3 tbsp (21 g) minced fresh ginger

3 tbsp (25 g) minced garlic

8 oz (225 g) ground plant-based protein of your choice, like Beyond Meat® or Impossible™, or ground pork

2 tbsp (30 ml) spicy bean sauce (I use the Lee Kum Kee brand)

⅔ cup (160 ml) low-sodium vegetable broth

2 tsp (5 g) cornstarch, mixed with ¼ cup (60 ml) warm water

1 lb (450 g) silken tofu, cut into 1-inch (2.5-cm) cubes

¼ cup (60 ml) Sichuan chili oil

¼ tsp sesame oil

¼ tsp granulated sugar

1–2 spring onions, sliced to serve

Turn on the rice cooker, set the mode to Cook and add the lid to let the rice cooker preheat for about 1 minute. Add the vegetable oil to the rice cooker, cover and give the oil 1 to 2 minutes to heat up. Then add the Sichuan peppercorns, ginger and garlic and sauté them for 30 seconds before adding the lid. Fry them for 1 to 2 minutes more, or until the garlic is lightly golden.

Toss in the plant-based protein and fry it for a minute. Cover and fry it for another 5 to 6 minutes, or until it's browned and cooked through. You might need a bit more time if you choose to use pork.

Now add the spicy bean sauce and stir it well for a few seconds. Pour in the broth and mix well. Cover and cook it for 2 to 3 minutes, until it comes to a simmer. Add the cornstarch slurry. Stir it well for a minute, or until the sauce starts to thicken. Now toss in the tofu and pour in the chili oil. Cook it for 2 to 3 minutes more. Stir in the sesame oil and sugar. Serve the dish with the sliced spring onions.

KOREAN CORN CHEESE

Is there a better combination than sweet corn and gooey mozzarella cheese? I first came across this dish at a Korean BBQ restaurant and totally fell in love. You can serve it as a snack with soju or strawberry milk. It works equally great as a side with some Korean-style ribs. Or you can use it as a dip with tortilla chips. It's so versatile. This corn and cheese casserole is seasoned with creamy mayonnaise and a little sugar and is cooked in melted butter, so it smells absolutely divine. I am using canned sweet corn for the dish which is already quite sweet but if you use fresh corn kernels, you might want to add some more sugar.

 Yield: 4 servings

14 oz (400 g) canned sweet corn, drained

¼ cup (40 g) diced bell peppers

3 tbsp (45 ml) mayonnaise

2 tsp (10 g) granulated sugar

Salt and freshly ground black pepper, to taste

3 tbsp (42 g) unsalted butter

1 cup (112 g) shredded mozzarella cheese

1 tsp cayenne pepper, to serve

1 tbsp (3 g) chopped scallions, to serve

In a medium-sized bowl, mix together the sweet corn, bell peppers, mayonnaise, sugar, salt and pepper.

Turn on the rice cooker, set the mode to Cook and add the lid to let the rice cooker preheat for about 1 minute. Add the butter to the rice cooker pot. Put the lid on and give the butter 1 to 2 minutes to begin melting.

As the butter melts, add the corn mixture to the pot. Cook it for 1 to 2 minutes, stirring constantly. Then stir in the mozzarella and let it cook, covered, for another 4 to 5 minutes, or until the cheese has melted. Stir it midway through. Season it with salt.

Serve the corn cheese with a sprinkle of cayenne pepper and scatter some chopped scallions over top.

SPANISH CHORIZO IN RED WINE

Chorizo is my favorite item on a charcuterie board. It's garlicky, smoky and rich, and I love it in sandwiches, stews, pastas and on its own as a cured meat.

This classic tapas dish of chorizo al vino is packed with flavor and so easy to make. I tried it first in Granada in southern Spain and found it so incredibly rich and delicious—these succulent discs of chorizo are served in a sticky red wine sauce. While this is more popular as an appetizer, it can be served as a main, too. Just double up the portions and serve it with some fresh bread and salad on the side.

 Yield: 4 servings

1 tbsp (15 ml) extra virgin olive oil

1 lb (450 g) chorizo, cut up into bite-sized pieces

⅓ cup (55 g) chopped white onions

1 tsp finely chopped garlic

1 bay leaf

1½ cups (360 ml) red wine

2 tbsp (30 ml) honey

1 tbsp (4 g) chopped flat-leaf parsley, to serve

Turn on the rice cooker, set the mode to Cook and add the lid to let the rice cooker preheat for about 1 minute.

Add the olive oil to the rice cooker pot and put the lid on. Give it 1 to 2 minutes to heat. Once the oil has heated up, add the chorizo pieces and fry, with the lid on, until they're golden brown. This should take about 3 to 4 minutes on each side. Then remove the chorizo and drain it on a paper towel–lined plate. Set it aside.

Add the onions, garlic and bay leaf to the rice cooker pot. Fry them, with the lid on, for 5 to 6 minutes, or until the onions are soft and translucent. Now return the chorizo to the pot and mix everything together well. Pour in the red wine and close the lid. Cook for 5 to 7 minutes, or until the wine reduces by almost half.

Add in the honey, give it a good stir and cook for another 4 to 5 minutes. At this stage, you will notice the wine has almost become syrupy.

Dish out the chorizo and the reduced wine into serving bowls and scatter the chopped parsley on top.

BRUNCH

Brunch is definitely my favorite meal. It combines the best of breakfast and lunch—sweet or savory, crunchy or saucy—and the options are endless. Brunch also gives you the license to eat for hours—you have the luxury of sleeping in and enjoying your meal at your leisure over the course of an afternoon. Plus, you can wash it all down with Bloody Marys and mimosas and feel classy while you're at it.

In this chapter, I am including easy-to-prep brunch dishes, which are ideal for entertaining a group of friends on the weekend or for a Monday morning treat to help alleviate the blues. You've got big Fluffy Pancakes with Berries and Cream (page 138). Or you can go for some of the eggy dishes like a Middle Eastern Shakshuka (page 141), with eggs poached in a peppery tomato sauce, or maybe a Gooey Cheddar and Asparagus Frittata (page 145). If you're after something healthier, you'll be glad to know that rice cookers are great for cooking oats and polenta, so I've also included some filling, nourishing porridges in this chapter too. Regardless of whether you like to kick off your day with sweet or savory, you'll have an array of options to choose from to upgrade your brunch game!

And it turns out the rice cooker is a neat little device that can make your brunch prep game a whole lot easier. It keeps the temperature even, so you won't have to watch over the stovetop for your porridge. Or if you are making eggy dishes, the rice cooker is great for cooking many eggs in one go, and you can boil, poach or scramble them all in the cooker. This is especially easy to do in rice cookers with a timer as you can get real precision for soft, runny yolks. But my favorite brunch dish made in the rice cooker is perhaps the pancake—the batter is cooked evenly throughout and you get guaranteed fluffiness each time.

FLUFFY PANCAKES
WITH BERRIES AND CREAM

The only thing better than fluffy pancakes are *giant* fluffy pancakes! Nothing says blowout brunch more than a tall stack of fresh, warm pancakes served with soft whipped cream and fresh berries, plus a generous drizzle of maple syrup. With its size, texture and taste, this rice cooker pancake is probably closer to a soft, delicious sponge cake than to an actual pancake—and I can't imagine what could possibly be better than eating cake for breakfast! Furthermore, you don't even have to bother flipping these pancakes, as the rice cooker cooks them evenly throughout, meaning your brunch prep is fuss-free and fun! If that sounds of interest to you, then you'll have to give these rice cooker pancakes a go.

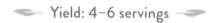 Yield: 4–6 servings

For the Pancake

7 oz (200 g) self-rising flour

1½ tsp (5 g) baking powder

1 tbsp (15 g) golden caster sugar

Pinch of salt

3 large eggs

2 tbsp (30 ml) melted salted butter, plus some more to grease the rice cooker

1 cup (240 ml) whole milk

For the Toppings

½ cup (120 ml) heavy cream, kept cold

2 tbsp (30 g) granulated sugar

Fresh berries (strawberries, blueberries, raspberries)

1 tbsp (8 g) powdered sugar

Maple syrup, to taste

In a large bowl, mix the self-rising flour, baking powder, caster sugar and salt together. Create a well in the center, then add the eggs, melted butter and milk. Whisk them together until you have a smooth batter.

For this recipe, there is no need to preheat the rice cooker. Just grease the rice cooker pot with some melted butter, then pour in the batter. You don't want to go above the halfway point as you need to allow space for the pancake to rise.

Cover and cook it for 45 minutes. It is likely that after the first 25 minutes or so, the cooker will automatically go to Warm. But that's absolutely fine—just leave it on Warm for another 15 to 20 minutes, or until the pancake is fully cooked. You can check it by inserting a toothpick and seeing if it comes out clean. Then use a spatula or simply invert the pancake onto a plate.

For the whipped cream topping, in a medium-sized bowl, whisk together the cream and granulated sugar until firm peaks form, about 4 to 5 minutes. Add a generous dollop of the whipped cream onto the pancake. Garnish it with the fresh berries, a dusting of powdered sugar and a drizzle of maple syrup.

MIDDLE EASTERN SHAKSHUKA

Shakshuka is made by gently poaching eggs in a simmering mixture of tomatoes and peppers, which originated in Tunisia but is now popular throughout the Middle East. I like to use a combination of fresh tomatoes and canned ones as it gives you more texture. Using only fresh tomatoes can make the dish a bit too watery, while the use of tomato puree alone makes it a tad too sweet for my taste.

What I love about shakshuka is how it's a blank canvas of a recipe that you can customize with spices, vegetables and toppings depending on whatever your mood calls for! I'm using paprika, cumin and harissa, but you can add cinnamon or coriander. Toppings can be just as versatile, ranging from chopped parsley to sour cream.

Yield: 2 servings

3 tbsp (45 ml) extra virgin olive oil, plus more for drizzling

¾ cup (120 g) thinly sliced red onions

¾ cup (110 g) thinly sliced red peppers

2 tbsp (17 g) minced garlic

2 tbsp (20 g) paprika

1 tsp chili powder

½ tbsp (8 g) harissa

2 tsp (8 g) cumin powder

1 cup (150 g) cherry tomatoes, halved

1½ cups (360 g) canned tomatoes

Salt, to taste

2–3 medium eggs

Avocado, feta and parsley, to serve (optional)

Turn on the rice cooker, set the mode to Cook and add the lid to let the rice cooker preheat for about 1 minute.

Add the olive oil to the rice cooker pot, cover and let the oil heat up for 1 to 2 minutes, then add the onions and sliced peppers to the pot. Sauté them for a minute and then cover and fry them for 5 to 6 minutes, or until the onions are golden brown.

Now add the garlic, paprika, chili powder, harissa and cumin. Fry them for 1 to 2 minutes, or until they're fragrant. Add the cherry tomatoes and canned tomatoes. Use the back of a spoon to crush the tomatoes. Season them with salt and cook, covered, for 8 to 10 minutes, or until the sauce thickens.

In the rice cooker, make some wells in the tomato mixture with a spoon and add the eggs. Put on the lid and steam for 6 to 8 minutes, or until the eggs are set. Serve it with the avocado, feta, parsley and a drizzle of olive oil, if desired.

AUTUMNAL APPLE PIE OATMEAL

What better way to start off the day than with a delicious take on comforting, lightly spiced apple pie that is also protein-rich and high in fiber? This oatmeal is equally perfect served warm on a cold winter day as it is served chilled in summer. And the best part is that it's ready in just 15 minutes! I recommend using a combination of different apples if possible, like Fuji, Granny Smith and Braeburn, so that you get a blend of sweet and tart flavors as well as a variety of textures.

⟋ Yield: 1 serving ⟍

For the Applesauce

3 cups (360 g) apples, peeled, cored and chopped

1 tsp granulated sugar

1 tsp lemon zest

1 tsp lemon juice

For the Oats

⅓ cup (30 g) rolled oats

1½ cups (180 g) apples, peeled and chopped

1 tbsp (10 g) chia seeds

1 tsp ground cinnamon

¼ tsp ground nutmeg

½ tsp sea salt

1¼ cups (300 ml) whole milk, or more as needed

1½ tbsp (21 ml) maple syrup

½ cup (120 ml) applesauce, previously made

½ tsp pure vanilla extract

1 tsp fresh lemon juice (optional)

For the Toppings

1 small apple, sliced

2 tbsp (30 g) chopped walnuts

Coconut whipped cream

Granola

Cinnamon

For the applesauce, place the apples, along with just enough water to cover them, into the rice cooker pot. Add the sugar, lemon zest and lemon juice. Cover and set the device to Cook for 7 to 10 minutes. Turn the rice cooker off and let the mixture cool for 10 to 15 minutes before adding it to a blender. Blend until a smooth puree forms (or you can use a hand blender). Set it aside.

For the oats, dry out the rice cooker pot completely and then add in the oats, apples, chia seeds, cinnamon, nutmeg, salt, milk, maple syrup and applesauce. Combine them well. Add the rice cooker lid and cook everything for 10 to 15 minutes, until the oats soften. Make sure to stir it every 2 to 3 minutes. If your oats look too dry after the first 10 minutes, you can add more milk, stirring well, until reaching the desired consistency.

Now stir in the vanilla extract and lemon juice, if using. Mix them in well and then ladle the oats out into a bowl.

Serve it with one or more of the suggested toppings: sliced apples, walnuts, coconut whipped cream, granola and cinnamon.

GOOEY CHEDDAR
AND ASPARAGUS FRITTATA

Frittata is one of my all-time favorite dishes to make for breakfast or brunch. When I realized that I could make a frittata in a rice cooker, I was elated. The rice cooker frittata is quicker and easier than the oven-baked version—there's no need to preheat your oven. You just mix the ingredients, pour them into the pot and let the magic happen. This asparagus and cheddar frittata is a fresh and summery dish that's nourishing and tasty. The ricotta adds a lovely creaminess to the dish, while the cheddar makes it gooey. I've kept the dish vegetarian, but feel free to add a handful of diced cooked ham to the egg mix for a more filling option.

➤ Yield: 2–3 servings ➤

1 lb (450 g) asparagus, washed, trimmed and sliced

2 tbsp (30 ml) olive oil

¾ cup (120 g) sliced white onions

6 large eggs

2 tbsp (28 g) unsalted butter, melted

¼ cup (20 g) basil leaves, sliced, plus 2–3 leaves to serve

¼ cup (35 g) canned peas, drained

¼ cup (25 g) ricotta

½ cup (50 g) shredded cheddar cheese, divided

Salt and freshly ground black pepper, to taste

1 tsp grated Parmesan

Add 2 cups (480 ml) of water to the rice cooker. Put on the lid and set the device to Cook for 8 to 10 minutes, or until the water comes to a boil. Place the asparagus stalks in the steamer basket and let them steam for 7 to 10 minutes, or until they're done. You can tell they are done when the asparagus is easy to pierce with a fork, but not mushy.

Dry out the rice cooker pot completely. Turn on the rice cooker, set the mode to Cook and add the lid to let the rice cooker preheat for about 1 minute. Add in the olive oil. Put on the lid and give it a minute or two for the oil to heat up. Toss in the onions and fry them, covered, for 5 to 6 minutes, or until they are translucent. Now add the asparagus and sauté the vegetables for 2 to 3 minutes more.

In a medium-sized bowl, whisk together the eggs and melted butter. Add the chopped basil, peas, ricotta and ¼ cup (25 g) of the cheddar cheese and season with salt and pepper. Whisk well and pour the egg mixture into the rice cooker pot.

Sprinkle the remaining ¼ cup (25 g) of cheddar cheese evenly on top. Cover and cook the frittata for approximately 15 minutes, or until the eggs are set. When it's done, carefully remove the frittata from the rice cooker with a plastic spatula and put it on a plate. Serve it hot with a sprinkle of grated Parmesan and basil.

CHEESY POLENTA BREAKFAST BOWL

This creamy polenta breakfast dish is total comfort food. For those who haven't tried polenta, it's made from dried, ground maize and is most commonly used to make cornbread. I love polenta as a side instead of mashed potatoes, deep-fried into tasty polenta fries or for breakfast instead of oats. Polenta has this buttery, slightly sweet taste. You can serve it with some stewed plums or strawberries or drizzle some nut butter over it. But I like to make it into a savory bowl and top it with sautéed veggies and eggs. If you are feeling particularly lazy, just add a generous knob of salted butter and some pepper and you're sorted!

— Yield: 2 servings —

2 tbsp (30 ml) olive oil, divided, plus more to serve

2 oz (60 g) chorizo, chopped

1 cup (150 g) cherry tomatoes

3 tbsp (42 g) unsalted butter, divided

½ cup (80 g) canned sweet corn, drained

2 cups (480 ml) whole milk

½ cup (80 g) instant polenta

2 cups (480 ml) chicken broth

¼ cup (25 g) shredded cheddar cheese

¼ cup (25 g) grated Parmesan

Salt and freshly ground black pepper, to taste

Turn on the rice cooker, set the mode to Cook and add the lid to let the rice cooker preheat for about 1 minute. Add 1 tablespoon (15 ml) of the olive oil to the rice cooker, put the lid on and give the oil 1 to 2 minutes to heat up. Then add in the chorizo, put the lid back on and fry it for 5 to 6 minutes, or until the chorizo is crispy. Set it aside.

Add the remaining tablespoon (15 ml) of olive oil to the pot. Let the oil heat up for a minute, with the lid on. Then throw in the tomatoes, cover and cook them for 4 to 5 minutes, or until they are nice and blistered. Set them aside and keep them warm.

Now add 1 tablespoon (14 g) of butter into the pot, place on the lid and cook for a minute. Once it melts, add the sweet corn. Sauté it for 2 to 3 minutes and then set it aside.

Pour the milk, polenta, broth and the remaining 2 tablespoons (28 g) of butter into the rice cooker pot. Cover and cook them for 20 to 25 minutes, or until the polenta has absorbed all the liquid.

Now add in the cheddar and Parmesan and mix well. Change the rice cooker mode to Warm. Keep it on this setting until you're ready to serve. Season it with salt and pepper and serve it topped with the fried chorizo, sweet corn and tomatoes. Drizzle over some more olive oil, if desired.

DESSERTS

If I had to pick between a starter and dessert, I know I would pick dessert every single time. I have a major sweet tooth and no matter how stuffed I am after dinner, I always make space for dessert. It seems like the only fitting way to end a meal. What's great about desserts is that they are almost as satisfying and therapeutic to make as they are to eat. There is something so soothing about swirling your spatula through a bowl of melted chocolate or watching your cream turn into soft peaks as you whisk. As a bonus, they usually also smell amazing.

Making desserts in the rice cooker is great: minimal fuss and clean up. No need to preheat an oven or worry about your desserts burning. Just put the ingredients into the pot and let them slow cook into sumptuous sweet treats!

In this chapter, I am sharing recipes from around the globe that I love whipping up at dinner parties or for myself when I crave a little something sweet to go with my coffee. It seems everyone enjoys a good Indian curry, but our desserts definitely deserve love, too. So, I'm sharing a few of our family dessert recipes that my mum would often make on festivals like Fudgy Coconut Barfi (Indian Fudge) (page 161) and Buttery Carrot Halwa (page 158). I'm particularly a fan of the halwa, as it elevates the natural sweetness of carrots and is hands down the best way to eat them, in my humble opinion. Once you try this dessert, I guarantee you will not look at carrots the same way again!

You can also find recipes for Thai Sticky Mango Rice (page 153) and Rose and Pistachio Rice Pudding (page 150)—beautiful desserts I fell in love with during my travels across Asia and the Middle East. I've also included classics like Panna Cotta with Raspberry Coulis (page 154) and Chai-Spiced Pears with Mascarpone (page 157), which are utterly indulgent and bound to impress your guests. These were the recipes I most enjoyed creating and photographing for this work, so I do hope that you also enjoy making and eating them.

ROSE AND PISTACHIO RICE PUDDING

A rice pudding is one of the simplest, most delightful desserts out there. It's creamy, comforting and made with the humblest of ingredients. Most countries of the world have their own take on rice pudding. In Spain, you've got Arroz con Leche, which is spiked with cinnamon. The Germans make theirs with blackberries, while Indians prepare kheer infused with cardamom. I am sharing a version of the dessert that is inspired by flavors from the Middle East: rose, honey and pistachio.

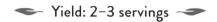 Yield: 2–3 servings

2 cups (480 ml) whole milk, plus more if needed

⅓ cup (66 g) pudding rice

¼ cup (50 g) granulated sugar

¼ tsp salt

1 cup (240 ml) coconut milk

¼ tsp orange zest

1 tsp rose water

½ cup (48 g) desiccated coconut

To Serve

Coconut flakes

Pistachios, crushed

Food grade rose petals

Dried strawberries or other berries

2 tsp (10 ml) honey

Add the milk, rice, sugar and salt to the rice cooker. Set the rice cooker to Cook. Put the lid on and let it simmer for 15 to 20 minutes, stirring every 5 or 6 minutes, until the rice is fully cooked. Take off the lid and give it all a good stir.

Then add in the coconut milk, orange zest, rose water and desiccated coconut. Mix it well. Feel free to add some more milk to thin out the pudding if you prefer. Turn the rice cooker mode to Warm and keep it in this mode until you're ready to serve it.

Ladle the rice pudding out into bowls and serve it with coconut flakes, pistachios, food grade rose petals and berries and drizzle it with honey.

THAI STICKY MANGO RICE

This classic Thai dessert, called Khao Niaow Ma Muang (which literally translates to Mango Sticky Rice), is as good as Thai street food gets. I do also enjoy other Thai street food delights like Pad See Eiw, Tom Yum Goong and Pad Kra Pao, but as someone with a serious sweet tooth, I feel that mango sticky rice is hard to beat. I love the velvety, glutinous rice topped with the creamy coconut sauce and sweet, fresh mango slices. It's a dessert that's undoubtedly tropical, rich and irresistible. The key to getting this dish just right is to use really thick coconut milk, the best quality mangoes you can find and Thai sweet or glutinous rice.

— Yield: 2 servings —

1 cup (200 g) Thai sticky rice or any other short-grain rice

1½ cups (360 ml) coconut milk

¼ tsp salt

1 tbsp (13 g) brown sugar

For the Topping

½ cup (120 ml) coconut cream

1 tbsp (8 g) cornstarch

4 tbsp (52 g) brown sugar

Pinch of salt

2 ripe mangoes, to serve

1 tsp black and white sesame seeds, to serve

Rinse the sticky rice five to seven times or until you're left with clear water. This step helps remove the excess starch that could make the rice gummy. Once you've rinsed it, leave the rice soaking in water for about 3 to 4 hours.

Now add the drained rice to the rice cooker pot. Add 1 cup (240 ml) of water. Cover and set the device to Cook. Give it 20 to 25 minutes, or until the rice is fully cooked. Remove the rice from the cooker pot, set it aside in a heatproof bowl or pot and keep it covered to stop it from drying out.

Turn off the rice cooker. Dry out the rice cooker pot completely and turn it back on.

Add in the coconut milk, salt and brown sugar. Set the rice cooker to Cook and keep stirring for 1 to 2 minutes. Then, cover and cook for 6 to 8 minutes, or until it comes to a boil. Once the mix comes to a boil, turn off the cooker and pour the coconut milk mixture into the bowl of rice, mixing until it is well incorporated. Allow it to cool.

For the topping, turn the rice cooker back on. Add the coconut cream into the rice cooker pot, along with the cornstarch, brown sugar and salt. Put on the lid and set the rice cooker to Cook. Cook it for 5 to 6 minutes, or until it comes to a gentle boil. Turn off the rice cooker.

In the meantime, peel and slice the mangoes.

Place the sticky rice on a plate, arrange the mangoes on the side and pour on the coconut cream topping. Sprinkle it with the sesame seeds.

PANNA COTTA WITH RASPBERRY COULIS

Panna cotta is an Italian dessert originating from the Piedmont region in Northern Italy and its name literally translates to cooked cream in Italian. It's a delicate, smooth and decadent dessert. Plus, I love how a well-set panna cotta wobbles—it's truly a delight for all the senses.

You can pair the panna cotta with poached fruits, wine syrups, baked plums, nuts and fresh herbs. Here I have opted for a raspberry coulis which is pretty, pink and just a little sharp to provide an enjoyable contrast to the creamy, rich panna cotta. This dessert is easy and pretty foolproof, but you need to make sure you're using the best quality heavy cream, natural vanilla bean and whole milk you can find.

〜 Yield: 4 servings 〜

For the Panna Cotta

3 sheets gelatin

1 cup plus 2 tsp (250 ml) whole milk

1 cup plus 2 tsp (250 ml) heavy cream

1 tsp vanilla extract

2 tbsp (30 g) granulated sugar

For the Raspberry Coulis

2 cups (250 g) fresh raspberries

2 tsp (10 g) granulated sugar

Pomegranate seeds, to serve

Fresh raspberries, to serve

For the panna cotta, in a small shallow bowl of cold water, soak the sheets of gelatin for 5 minutes to soften them. Set them aside.

Turn on the rice cooker. Place the whole milk, cream, vanilla and sugar into the pot. Set the rice cooker to Cook. Cover and let it heat up for 5 to 6 minutes, or until it comes to a simmer.

Squeeze the water out of the gelatin sheets and add them to the pot. Stir them for 4 to 5 minutes, or until the gelatin is dissolved. Turn off the rice cooker, then pour the mix into ramekins and let them set in a fridge for at least 5 hours or until they are set. I'm using 3 x 3 x 2-inch (7.5 x 7.5 x 5-cm) ramekins, but feel free to use bigger or smaller ramekins, keeping in mind that the number of servings might differ if you do.

To begin making the raspberry coulis, clean and dry out the rice cooker pot completely and then turn it on Cook again. Place the raspberries and sugar into the rice cooker pot. Cover and cook them for 5 to 6 minutes, or until the berries begin to collapse. You can puree the mix if you like and pass it through a mesh sieve to get out the seeds, but I like the additional texture the unblended coulis adds to the dish, so I use it as is.

Remove the coulis to a bowl. Chill it in the fridge for a few minutes so it doesn't melt the panna cotta when you pour it over the top.

Turn the panna cottas out onto your serving plates. If they seem stuck to the molds, just dip each mold very quickly (about 4 to 5 seconds) in hot water and then try turning them upside down onto the middle of a plate and give it a tap and a shake. Spoon the coulis over top and serve with a scattering of pomegranate seeds and fresh raspberries on the side.

CHAI-SPICED PEARS WITH MASCARPONE

Poached pears are such an elegant yet easy dessert. I am not usually a fan of fresh pears, but poached pears are a completely different story. Unlike most other fruits, pears are great at holding their shape during poaching and really transform in flavor, beautifully absorbing the spices and scents of the poaching liquid. Typically the longer you leave the pears in the syrup, the more tender and flavorsome they become.

I tend to make a fairly big batch that I can then refrigerate and enjoy over the course of a few days, be it with my bowl of porridge in the morning, with some sourdough and ricotta or as a tea-time treat with a drizzle of custard!

⟵ Yield: 4 servings ⟶

4 cups (960 ml) water

2 tbsp (5 g) Darjeeling loose leaf tea or 3 tea bags

1 cup (200 g) granulated sugar

1 tbsp (7 g) sliced fresh ginger

1 tsp fennel seeds

1 cinnamon stick

2 star anise

4 cardamom pods, cracked

4 firm pears, peeled

For the Whipped Mascarpone

¼ cup (50 g) mascarpone cheese

3½ oz (100 g) whipping cream, cold

2 tbsp (16 g) powdered sugar, sifted

¼ cup (35 g) toasted hazelnuts, roughly chopped, to serve

Place the water, tea, sugar, ginger, fennel seeds, cinnamon, star anise and cardamom pods into the rice cooker pot. Set the rice cooker to Cook and put the lid on. Give the syrup 8 to 10 minutes to come to a boil. Add the pears and then put the lid back on. Continue to simmer for 25 to 30 minutes, or until the pears are tender.

Remove the pears from the pot and set them aside. Let the poaching liquid simmer in the rice cooker pot for another 7 to 10 minutes, or until it reduces.

Strain the poaching liquid and discard the whole spices. Place the pears and the liquid in a container. Keep them in the fridge for a few hours or ideally overnight, to really let the flavors infuse.

When you're ready to serve, make the whipped mascarpone. Add the mascarpone cheese, whipping cream and powdered sugar to a bowl and whisk until fluffy. Place the poached pears on your serving plates. Sprinkle them with the toasted hazelnuts and add a generous dollop of the mascarpone cream on the side.

BUTTERY CARROT HALWA

This might just be my number one way of eating carrots: grated, slow-cooked in ghee and caramelized with milk and sugar. This popular dessert from India and Pakistan, also called Gajar ka Halwa, is a winter delicacy that taps into the natural sweetness of carrots and celebrates it. You can serve it hot or cold but I prefer having it hot with a cheeky scoop of ice cream on the side!

The hardest part of this dish is grating the carrots, but pre-shredded carrots will work equally well. I would advise going for young, orange carrots that are naturally sweeter and cook more easily. You also want to avoid as much of the core as possible when grating as that part of the carrot tends to be tougher.

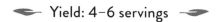 Yield: 4–6 servings

3 tbsp (45 g) ghee or 3 tbsp (42 g) salted butter

1 lb (450 g) carrots, peeled and grated

2 cups (480 ml) whole milk

½ cup (100 g) granulated sugar

2 tbsp (15 g) milk powder

Almond flakes and chopped pistachios, to serve

Turn on the rice cooker, set the mode to Cook and add the lid to let the rice cooker preheat for about 1 minute. Add the ghee to the rice cooker pot. Put on the lid and let it melt for 1 to 2 minutes.

Once melted, add the carrots. Fry them for 5 minutes, stirring constantly. Now add the lid and let them cook for 4 to 5 minutes with the lid on. Stir them midway through.

Pour in the milk and cook it for another 8 to 10 minutes, or until most of the milk has been absorbed. Make sure to stir midway through so the milk doesn't burn or stick to the bottom.

Now add the sugar and mix it well. Keep stirring until the sugar is fully incorporated. Stir in the milk powder. Finally, serve it with almond flakes and chopped pistachios.

FUDGY COCONUT BARFI (INDIAN FUDGE)

What I love about this dessert is that it requires very few ingredients and very little time. Whenever we'd have last-minute guests visiting or I pestered my mum for a sweet snack, this is what she'd make. Since coconut is considered to be auspicious, the barfi is also a common offering at Hindu festivals.

Coconut barfi is essentially a rich, Indian-style fudge with chewy, soft coconut. Freshly grated coconut works best but desiccated coconut will also do—just soak it in milk for a few minutes before using it. My recipe uses milk and sugar, but you can also use condensed milk if you want to cut down the cooking time even further.

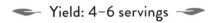 Yield: 4–6 servings

5 tbsp (75 g) ghee or 5 tbsp (70 g) salted butter, divided

⅓ cup (47 g) cashews

3 cups (285 g) coconut, freshly grated or desiccated

½ cup (120 ml) whole milk

2 cups (400 g) granulated sugar

1 tbsp (10 g) milk powder

Turn on the rice cooker, set the mode to Cook and add the lid to let the rice cooker preheat for about 1 minute.

Add 1 tablespoon (15 g) of ghee to the rice cooker pot. Put the lid on for 1 to 2 minutes, or until the ghee melts. Then add the cashews and sauté them for 30 seconds before putting the lid on and frying them for 3 to 4 minutes, or until they are lightly golden. Set them aside.

Add 3 tablespoons (45 g) of ghee to the pot and then add the coconut. Sauté it for a minute. Cover and fry the coconut for 4 to 5 minutes, stirring well. Once the coconut starts to turn golden brown, add the milk and sugar. Stir it well. Then cover and cook the mixture for 8 to 10 minutes, or until it thickens. Stir it midway through.

Now add the milk powder and stir it for a minute, or until the mix is dry and sticky.

Grease a container or tray with the remaining 1 tablespoon (15 g) of ghee and then add the coconut mixture to it. Use a spatula to smooth out the top. If you are using a tray, make sure to get one with slightly raised sides, or else the barfi won't have much height. We want to aim for a cubical shape where possible. But if you don't have a suitable container, you can also roll the mix with your hands into balls, which is the more traditional way of serving them in India.

Place one fried cashew on top of each barfi. It is important to complete this step before putting the barfi in the fridge because they solidify when they cool down, so the texture will be less malleable and you won't really be able to set the nuts in place.

Now let it set in the refrigerator for 1 to 2 hours. Then invert it onto a plate or tray and cut it roughly into squares before serving.

ACKNOWLEDGMENTS

I would have never dreamed of having my own cookbook a few years back, and I honestly pinch myself when I realize I have one now! Writing this cookbook has been an incredible yet challenging experience, and I am really grateful to every single person who made this happen.

Firstly, thank you to my publisher for giving me this amazing opportunity. In particular, I want to thank Emily Taylor for seeing the potential in me and for supporting me with editing this book very quickly and efficiently.

Thank you to Ha Le for the gorgeous photography and the wonderful styling.

Thank you to all my friends and followers who support my food blog—I wouldn't be here without you.

Special thanks to my mum for testing out several of my recipes, as well as for sharing many of her own beautiful recipes with me so I could recreate favorites from my childhood for this book. I definitely get my love for cooking and feeding others from her. Thank you to both my mum and dad for always backing me up and for inspiring me to be the best version of myself. I hope to make you proud.

ABOUT THE AUTHOR

Shree Mitra is the recipe creator and restaurant reviewer behind @truffleandtoast, which made it to Square Meal's list of London's best food blogs. Shree has been food blogging in London for the past 7 years and reviews a whopping 25 to 30 new London restaurants each month. But when she isn't eating out, she is busy experimenting in the kitchen and whipping up recipes for various brands like IKEA®, George Foreman®, KFC®, Heinz®, Sainsbury's, Old El Paso™ and Lee Kum Kee, as well as for tourism authorities of countries like Thailand and Malta. She also collaborated with celebrity chef Gordon Ramsay for the launch of his Burger restaurant in London's luxury retail establishment, Harrods. Beyond her love for cooking, Shree is also a self-confessed tech nerd with a computer science degree from the University of Cambridge and works in sustainability in her day job, where she has spent a lot of time exploring how the food industry in London can reduce its carbon footprint.

INDEX